THIS IS MY SONG, THIS IS MY STORY

THIS IS MY SONG, THIS IS MY STORY

I'm Not Who I Used To Be

TERRIE L. BROOM

ARPress
ILLUMINATING IDEAS,
EMPOWERING VOICES

ARPress
45 Dan Road Suite 5
Canton MA 02021
Hotline: 1(888) 821-0229
Fax: 1(508) 545-7580

Ordering Information:
Quantity sales. Special discounts are available on quantity purchases by corporations, associations, and others. For details, contact the publisher at the address above.

Printed in the United States of America.

ISBN-13:   Softcover   979-8-89389-879-8
                  eBook   979-8-89389-880-4

Library of Congress Control Number: 2024923848

TABLE OF CONTENTS

DEDICATIONS

I want to dedicate this book to the Glory of God my Father who never gave up on me and never ran out on me, who left the ninety-nine and came after me.

****

I want to acknowledge and thank Beth Anderson for intentionally walking into my life and demonstrating Jesus and accepting me as I was and encouraging me to grow next step after next step.

****

I want to acknowledge and thank Drenda Marchman, who even thou would speak tough love in my struggle with diabetes often came to my rescue, a real lifesaver!

****

I want to thank Nancy Andrews and Chris Lacek for being proactive Small Group leaders by going the extra step to get in touch with a counselor to work out my need for deeper healing.

****

I want to thank my Counselor (which wanted to not be named to keep her anonymity) who loved, discipled and counseled me into a deeper relationship with God, who taught me about

1

the "Father Ladder" that changed the way I see and Know relationship with the Trinity.

****

I want to thank Wendy Speaks for being a true friend, even when it meant she had to walk away for a couple of seasons and trust Father God in what was going on in my life, friend friends don't drag you into sin.

****

Thank you Kim Copeland, for being a friend and sister in the faith and for the support you extended me and for the encouragement to do the Father's will.

****

Finally I would like to thank Sallie Brassfield for all the deep conversations, times and roads we shared in this journey to the depths of our Father's Heart.

"Therefore, since we have this ministry, as we receive mercy, We do not lose heart, but we renounce the things hidden because of shame, not walking in craftiness, or adulterating The word of God, but by the manifestation of Truth Commending ourselves to every man's conscience in the sight of God." 2 Corinthians 4:2

FROM THE AUTHOR

I have always loved music. Whenever I was depressed or lonely I would always listen to my favorite songs for hours at a time. I always got drawn in by the lyrics and they would touch something deep in my soul.

There came a time when God would reach out to me through the music I was listening to, often telling me the opposite of what I was hearing. As I tell my story I look back and include the music and songs and lyrics that touched me as I was on my journey into the heart of God.

This is a book the Lord led me to write and it is different than any other book I have ever read. This is an interactive book that you can look up the songs on YouTube and play back before or after each chapter. These are the songs that testify of my state of being and my progress along my journey.

I hope it ministers to you and encourages you to see that change is possible if you choose to believe, confess your sin, repent and trust a loving Father who is the Almighty.

1 Corinthians 6:9-11; Do you not know that the unrighteous will not inherit the kingdom of God? Do not be deceived; neither fornicators, nor idolaters, nor adulterers, nor effeminate, nor homosexuals nor thieves, nor the covetous, nor drunkards, nor revilers, nor swindlers, will inherit the kingdom of God.

Such were some of you; but you were washed, but you were sanctified, but you were justified in the name of the Lord Jesus Christ and in the Spirit of our God. (NAS)

I BELIEVE

I want to share a true story, not just a story but a true life story better than Lifetime story made for TV.

I want to say from the onset that there are many people who struggle with same sex attractions, gender identity issues and homosexuality. This is my story, and God is not prejudiced, this could be your story too, if the shoe doesn't fit, just kick it off, God, he causes the sun to rise on the evil and the good, and sends rain on the righteous and the unrighteous. (Matt. 5:45)

It was 2003, I had just turned thirty-nine years old. I was living and loving life largely. I had just started a new job as a service writer, I had been selling automobiles for the last ten years.

After years of struggling to accept myself as a lesbian I had finally found the love of my life and with our pets as our "children" we were as settled as settle could be for us. Except for the fact my parents didn't agree with my lifestyle, and my partner's mom was not excited about our relationship as well, all was good. Now my brother who was fifteen months younger than me, well, he was happy about me coming out, he had been living in the closet for a long time except to his close friends.

Yes, life was great, all was good and as they say," life is full of fun and giggles until someone gets hurt, then it's a total different story.

It was the beginning of October and I had almost forgotten it was coming up on my brother Tom's birthday. Here it was October the 5th and his birthday was in two days. Luckily I had a computer at work and could get online and shop for him, but I didn't have time to shop I had better think of something fast so I could get it shipped in time for him to get it ON his birthday. It occurred to me he loved fresh flowers. He always had fresh flowers in his house especially when I came or anyone came to visit him. So I thought I haven't bought him anything in a while and I usually don't spend a lot on birthday gifts and rarely did I spend over twenty-five dollars on something that was fading by the hours but this day I opted to spend seventy-five dollars on flowers, autumn flowers too which meant probably half of it was made out of dead sticks. Looking back on it now I am sure glad I spent the money and bought the largest bouquet.

It was only six weeks later and I was trying to catch up with my brother Tom to ask him his opinion on buying a house. My partner and I had been living together for four years now, we had the "commitment ceremony" to seal our relationship and now we were looking for a bigger house than the townhouse we were living in. I had called Tom because we always bounced off ideas and confided in each other about life and the opportunities that might be available for us. I had tried to call him several times and left messages on his voicemail twice. It was getting real close to Thanksgiving, so I thought that he and his partner may be vacationing or going somewhere to see his partner's family for the holiday.

I think it was on Wednesday that I told my partner (let's just call her name Kayla) that if he doesn't call by Friday, we are driving to Atlanta and knocking on his door. This is so highly unusual for him not to call me back especially when I left a voicemail on his phone about some family gossip...surely he would have called me back on that alone.

Well Thanksgiving came and went; Kayla and I ate at my folk's house and mother did ask if I had heard from Tom, (because Tom had cut my mother and father off ten years before over a huge offense.) I told her I had not, but I had called him several times and was probably going to go see him tomorrow when I got off work.

The next day, Friday at work I was thinking if he doesn't call me I am leaving and going to drive right on up there and figure out if he is out of town or what. It was about nine o'clock a.m. and my cell phone began ringing and it read "Tom", I was so excited I almost dropped my cell phone! I answered and, said "Tom"! Then I heard the voice on the other end and it was Winston, my brother's life partner. He said," Terrie, this is Winston, and I know you must feel like we were ignoring you and we kinda were. But that was what Tom wanted." I said, "What is going on what has happened was he in an accident is he in the hospital is he okay?" I was just shooting up all these questions that had been piling up in my mind for days and days, and then Winston said," are you sitting down"? And I was telling him they don't let us sit down here at work just tell me! That's when he just pretty much blurted it out, "Tom died yesterday at one o'clock." I mean hearing that was so surreal, all the noise in the service department just went silent and I couldn't hear anything, I could not believe what I was hearing.

Winston went on to tell me that they thought they had his medical issues straighten out and was getting out of the woods, it was hard for my brother to decide to go into the hospital he had saved up sick days that amounted up to six weeks and was talked into checking into the hospital as like a time of "spa treatment" to reset and balance his system out. Unfortunately Tom didn't get to use up his sick days. Tom had died of complications to Aids and developed cancer in his colon. He had been hiding the fact that he had Aids for eighteen years, not even telling his closest friends that were also dying with Aids, he never told anyone not even me. I was shocked, overwhelmed and taken for a loop as they say. Winston did say he was hoping Tom would come out of his coma because he knew we had both grown closer in recent years and wanted permission against what Tom had said in the past about notifications once he got bad.

This is where my whole world turned upside down. Life was fun until this happened.

Looking back, Tom must have known he was getting worse, our conversations seemed to be getting much deeper and meaningful. A couple of months before, we really talked about our childhood, the good, the bad and the ugly. He was so jealous of my athletic abilities and how easy it was for me to make lifetime friends. I told him I was jealous of how he could study and be so smart and how he could put an outfit together and color coordinate so well. I was a goofball and He was Mr. Wonderful. I remember how we laughed out loud at each other and also found ourselves holding back tears too.

I had never had anyone that was close to me die, oh my great uncles and aunts, my grandparents but they were old it seemed normal. To have your sibling die that was fifteen months younger than you will get your attention real fast. I must have cried everyday going to work and coming home from work for over a year. When I would be driving I would listen to the radio and every time I heard this song, "I Believe" by Diamond Rio I would just melt, it would be my song of remembrance to Tom, and I so wanted to believe.

(Okay, this is where you can go to YouTube and look up the song "I Believe")

Tom and I around 2000 Gay Pride in Atlanta, GA.

One of the last Holidays we got to spend together before Tom passed away.

CHAPTER TWO

I AM the Only One

Life had forever changed me. Time, to me seemed to stand still. My thoughts were overwhelming me and I could not process much of what was coming to my mind. I felt like I lost my best friend. I would for months have this reoccurring nightmare about a story in the Bible, it is in the book of Luke, about a rich man who use to come and go with his wealthy self and walk right by this poor man named Lazarus, who was laid by his gate day after day. This poor man, sitting, just begging for the crumbs from the rich man's table, even the dogs would sit and lick the poor man's sores.

Well as the story goes, the poor man Lazarus died and was carried off by angels to the bosom of Father Abraham and as it would be too the rich man died and it says he was just buried, he was in Hades and looking far away and up from there he could see Lazarus in the bosom of Abraham. The rich man who now is being tormented cried out to Father Abraham for mercy and asked if he would send Lazarus with a drop of water from the tip of his finger to quench his thirsty tongue for the flames were too much. Father Abraham responded to the rich man and said, "Child, remember that during your life you received good things and likewise Lazarus bad things; but now he is being comforted here and you are in agony."

I tell you who is in agony! Me! Just the thought of my brother who by all appearances could very well be just like this rich man. Tom was very wealthy and he dressed for the best and put down others who didn't live to the standard he was accustomed. Don't get me wrong he was generous to some, those who he wanted to impress which were his friends or friends of family members.

But I was totally being tormented day after day thinking my brother is in hell, and if he is in hell, well what about me? Was I going to hell, was being gay really a sin? I thought I had put all those questions to rest years ago, but now with my brother's death it was stirring up doubts.

For me, whenever I was sad or lonely I would drown out the world by listening to music it just seemed to do something to my soul. I was listening to my music and it seemed God was reaching out to me through the songs I would be listening to, at the time I was listening to Melissa Etheridge singing "I am the Only One". This song speaks about wanting someone that looks good to you," go on and hold her, hold her till she tells you nothing is wrong, but I will be the only one who walk across the fire for you, I will be the only one who will drown in my desire for you, when all your promises are gone I am the only one."

It was like I could hear God saying to me that He was the only one for me, and he would walk across the fire for me and yet I come to find out he had done much, much more than that for me and I would soon come to understand and realize just how much he would go through just to reach me.

The rest of that story in Luke, says after Father Abraham told the rich man that even if he wanted to come quench his thirst he couldn't for there was a barrier between hades and paradise. With that said, the rich man begged for Father Abraham to send someone to go to his five other brothers to warn them of this place he ended up at, for not even the rich man wished hell for his brothers.

Father Abraham told him his brothers has the same opportunity he had, they have Moses and the prophet's words, but even the rich man thought that was not enough, but even Father Abraham said they would not even believe if someone came back from dead to warn them of the Truth.

I started on an internal journey you might say. I began searching for something to soothe my aching and wounded soul. I would cry out to God to let me know if my brother was okay, I needed a sign or some kind of answer to my questions of his eternal fate. It was about six months after his death I had a great dream.

I dreamed that my parents and I were visiting Tom's house, since my parents never got to see how much he and Winston had put so much work into that house, it looked like a mini botanical garden with a pool a perfect oasis, as I mentioned before, they hadn't seen or talked to each other in ten years.

So, as we three came up to his house Winston opened the door and we walked in around the foyer following Winston's lead through the living room and I was in the rear of my folks, as we came through there I could see Tom sitting on the couch all dressed in his fine preppy clothes, I noticed he was barefoot and it seemed no one else noticed him sitting there, only me.

As they preceded on through the dining room and out to the kitchen, I was looking right at Tom and he was smiling and he reached out to me with his barefoot tagging me in a playful way as he had done several times before when we were children.

I said, Tom, what are you doing here and where have you been?! Then he looked at me and smiled and he was so excited to tell me that I was right about when I use to talk about Heaven, except it was much much more than I had any idea about. I said what is it like and are you okay? He told me to not worry or grieve over him anymore, that he was fine, and that there were no words in our language to even describe what Heaven is like only that It was more than I could ever imagine and I would be okay, and to just know that he was okay, then I just woke up with no fear anymore in my heart but a calmness and surety that I believed Tom had made it to Heaven, and that God gave me that dream to relieve my broken heart.

Some months passed and I had heard through some friends that one of my old friends, Ellen, I use to go to church with was gifted with dream interpretation, so I jumped at the chance to reconnect with her to see if she would interpret my dream for some confirmation. I contacted her through Facebook and asked her if she minded to hear one of my dreams and to interpret it. So I sent her a message with just the dream, and she responded as follows:

Thanks for giving me a shot at your dream. This is a great dream…and it IS from your Daddy! When you were in that tail spin after Tom's death, you cried out to your Daddy. He heard you and because he loves you so much he gave you this dream to answer your questions.

I don't know Tom so I couldn't tell you a thing about his relationship, or lack of relationship with God, but God knew. Just like Tom hid his illness there were probably things you never knew about Tom in his quest for truth and God.

But… God knew.

God is always speaking but we don't always recognize that He is. Dreams can bring answers to our questions or warnings or even foretell what is ahead of you.

A house represents one's life because after all, home is where the heart is. A house represents your identity; your roots. When you saw Tom he was dressed in his usual fine way…meaning he had a "covering" of righteousness. His bare feet indicates that there was no walk with the Lord. He was sitting on a couch which means that he had come to a place of rest. I believe that somehow, Tom found God and had given his heart to Him but that he just never walked out a relationship with Him. Your right about salvation when you told me it's not about what you do but who you know.

Ellen then told me, Terrie God loves you so much he actually sent Tom to you in your dream to let you know that he really did make it to Heaven. Tom was telling you that there's no way for your earthly mind to understand what is waiting for you there. Tom's playful way with you was a message that all is well and you can be at peace because he is.

There's more.

Your parents were there as well and they headed to the dining room. A dining room is where food is served…in this case it is spiritual food. They are beginning to be hungry for God… which is why they headed directly for the dining room. They, too, have had many questions about Tom.

As I was reading all of this it was setting so well in my heart and brought great comfort and peace to know that God heard me cry out to Him for answers and by His great grace gave me a dream like that and that I would have an opportunity to have it interpreted, it meant so much to me that I will never forget it. Thanks Ellen!

This was just the beginnings of how my life would turn up-side down, my life as I knew it was soon to be shaken to its foundations and the scales would soon fall off mine eyes as well.

What I thought of as living the dream would soon be a reckoning of giant proportions to the very core beliefs and ideals I had chosen to believe and live for, until I started seeking out to have an encounter with a living God.

CHAPTER THREE

I am worn (Tenth Avenue North)

This song, "I am Worn" I taught it to myself on the guitar and I would sit in my little office in my house and play it over and over again. This is where I was. I was overwhelmed, emotionally exhausted, discouraged and totally feeling like I had failed in life.

My partner had just changed jobs and started a general management position at Starbucks. She was busy learning that business putting in the hours giving three hundred percent of her attention to it and then coming home to me and our dogs.

I was driving thirty minutes to and from my work, and on Fridays it never failed there would be a wreck on I- 459, which made it even a longer commute. We decided since our careers were going great and we were doing so well that we would build a house in a prestigious neighborhood, it would be our dream house. I even went to my bosses and asked if there was any foreseen reason why I would not be able to continue working for them.

The economy was booming and it seemed we were all building or buying houses at my work, life was good.

While we were working hard and making good income we did play too. We often took mini trips to the beach, we would travel and even got the chance to go to England for a cruise that Kayla's parents planned for the family. Life was getting back to normal. Kayla and I seemed so content, her with her career and me with my career. I wanted to laugh again feel good again, love again.

For a while when I was working in commission sales I would gamble at the casinos. We had one only two and half hours away if you drove like eighty miles an hour. It was not a bad drive and I had been going there when selling cars didn't provide enough income, my little brother who worked with me he would go also, just to try to make a decent living and it worked out for us a lot of times.

We were great at playing crapps. It was almost like we had ESP. Then eventually, I would go every weekend, the first year I made like thirty thousand dollars just playing on the weekends, I won a lot the first couple of years and it got me addicted to the feeling and it filled a void I was missing for a while. I tried to fill this void myself, through gambling or with emotional and sometimes physical dependent relationships.

I was starting to be full of myself acting arrogantly, bragging all the time, demanding a lot from people around me I would work hard and play hard. Like I mentioned Kayla's dad invited the whole family and significant others (that would be me) to go on a wonderful trip, a barge cruise on the River Thames in England. Well I had been working as a service writer now for over two years and I was due for a two week vacation, but my boss had the gall and nerve to tell me I couldn't take all of it at one time. I was so arrogant I told him I was looking for a job when I accepted this job and I was going on this trip of a lifetime whether he approved it or not.

He came back a few hours later saying the owner wanted to see my itinerary. Really? No, it was him who wanted to see what we were doing and if it actually was going to take 14 days to do this trip. I could not believe he wanted to see our itinerary.

There was another time, I wasn't too proud of, where I had Kayla's family coming into town for a short visit, they lived in Minnesota so we did not get to see them very much. I came into work, which is a commissioned paying job mind you and I asked my manager if I could possibly leave early Thursday because of family coming into town. His response was no, I don't think we can do that…which my response was, I was asking but I guess I am now telling you I am taking off at twelve Thursday and I will not be back til Monday and I'll be glad to sign any write up on me for my file then.

Everyone's jaw dropped they couldn't believe I would say that to the boss. But I did and I did take off. No wonder when the economy bubble busted in 2008 I was like one of the first to be laid off. I guess it is very true what the Bible says about pride; "pride goes before destruction, a haughty spirit before a fall." (Proverbs 16:18).

CHAPTER FOUR

There is nothing greater than grace

What do you do when you're given the pink slip? It was the first week of December in 2008 and the economy was plummeting the housing market bubble has just popped and we just knew it was a matter of time before we all felt the effects of this economic crash.

I got called into the office by my supervisor and manager and was told that they appreciated how I worked and no fault to anyone, decisions had to be made and in no way am I being fired but just laid off. I was the last service writer to be hired so with seniority I was the first one to be the first to be let go. They gave me a check a little severance pay and a handshake and a promise of a letter of reference if I should need one.

I couldn't believe it but then again, I saw it coming. A few months earlier Kayla and I decided to downsize everything we could from trading- in our sports car for a gas saver to buying me a "Scooby Doo" van that was 22yrs. Old, one of my good customers offered it to me for like 2000.00, paid cash for that and then we got rid of the new motorcycle I had bought the year before; if that wasn't enough we went further to changing to basic cable and no more eating out we literally would eat at home and meet our friends at restaurants and just have a drink.

We did everything we could to try to keep the new house we had just built just 3 years ago and now I had been laid off. To make matters worse I had a friend of mine who I had known for years we were pretty close. When I came out of the closet and embraced the gay lifestyle she broke fellowship with me and pulled away. I always tried to stay in touch during holidays and birthdays by sending cards or leaving voicemails. She had just called me last week and told me "God" had told her she needed to deliver me a message to me, and crying on the phone she said she could not ignore what He was asking her to do, my blood may be on her hands if she did not obey this directive.

Well, she got my attention, so I was like so what is the message? She said if you don't repent, you're going to die. Okay, so we are all gonna die, someday. She said this is serious, you will die, says the Lord, prematurely if you do not repent. I was thinking yeah, uh I think you are off your bi-polar medicine and I will just file that away as my friend loves me and means well; she is just trying to scare the "hell" out of me. I kindly said okay thanks for that" word" I got to go and hung up the phone.

Driving home that night I began thinking about that conversation. I said something to the effect to The Lord like, I don't know what you are doing to me but I am willing to listen if you are trying to get my attention.

I was talking to my friend and mentor from high school days; Sallie, she knew me better than anyone and had seen me struggle to find my place in this world. She was the first one I ever told about my attractions to the same sex and who I confessed to when I eventually got involved with someone for the first time. Sallie had always been there for me to talk things through.

Sallie, this particular time was telling me of a pastor who was preaching some great truths she had been hungry to hear. He was on TV, he was from Singapore.

She suggested for me to watch and listen to him so I did. I started to watch him every day; since I was laid off work just collecting my unemployment I had time to watch and listen, take time and start looking into spiritual things. The more and more I listen to Pastor Joseph Prince the more my eyes seem to see and understand.

I had gotten his book "Destine to Reign" and read it through in about a week. For the first time I was beginning to see that I had misinterpreted the whole meaning of Grace. I actually thought if God loved me He would understand my choices in life and would not hold it against me. I also thought he made me who I was and if I had the faith to believe he would accept me, he would receive me just as I was in my truth of being gay, and to lie about being gay would be "unnatural" for me trying to justify Romans chapter one of course. I started listening to Joseph Prince on a regular basis. I learned a lot about who Jesus is and how he came to redeem the world and to make us righteous how He came to exchange His life for our lives to bring us out of darkness and into His light.

I really was taking it all in and would try to get Kayla to watch this with me, but he, Joseph being from Singapore, had a small dialect issue and it was hard for Kayla to follow him. Strange thing was I could understand every word he was saying. So as you can guess I was watching this and she was in another room watching something else.

As things were going our friends were really draining on us. They complained all the time never happy always wanting to party it up drink a lot and never happy. One couple actually caught there house on fire not once but twice losing all their belongings, and then living it up replacing everything with insurance money. Some of our friends were addicted to drugs others to alcohol. Then there were the irresponsible friends who drove drunk and to seem always be totaling out their cars.

Kayla and I were both getting tired of this drama always going on. I told her we should start going to church just to find normal decent people to be friends with, not to imply that people who go to church don't have any drama but hopefully they would be better off than our friends were.

It just so happened I ran into a friend from when I was in my teens that was going to a huge mega church, Church of the Highlands. She had invited Kayla and me to come and visit. I wasn't sure about it at first but she told us she was leading a small bible study at her home and that we should come and visit. It seemed like a small step to take to get involved in meeting some new people and after discussing it with Kayla we agreed to visit the small group as they called it. When we arrived it was like an old familiar feeling from my youth when I use to go to bible study every week. Just to hear people pray seemed to warm my heart. The study was comfortable and it was not hard talking and getting to know everyone. On the weekends some of us would meet up to watch college football games, we would on other weekends cook out, it was a real bonding time to get to know these people.

After a while, we slowly started to acclimate to attending the church itself. I had been hurt by the church in my early twenty's and was not sure about getting involved again, but I did miss the worship music and feeling the presence of God; that I believe is what I was searching for in my heart of hearts.

One day I woke up not feeling well, I felt drained and exhausted and there was this continual thrushing sound going on inside my head like I could hear my own pulse. I just kind of ignored it for days and weeks. I was not able to sleep well because I kept hearing this thrushing pumping noise in my head all the time. We had planned on having a party at our house we called it a" Facebook friend party".

I had friends coming from out of town from high school to others across town and neighbors anyone and everyone was invited it was a great time in spring to cook out. I was really feeling even worse than I had been this day just walking around SAM's was about to exhaust me to the point Kayla wanted to cancel the party but we had some guest coming from out of town and so I told her not to cancel, for us to do it and I would take it easy.

Well after the party that night, I went to bed, but I got up like at two o'clock in the morning and I went to the bathroom I felt awful, and then I just dropped a ton of blood all at once. I went and woke up Kayla and said "something is really wrong, you got to get up and help me get dressed and take me to the emergency room!" She got up went to the bathroom saw all the blood and got really excited and was upset and started to get her and myself dressed and she drove like a bat out of hell to get me to the ER and I thought I was gonna die before we got there over her driving!!

I was able to walk into the emergency room and when I did the couple of people behind the counter saw me coming in and they dropped their clip boards and said I don't know what's wrong with you but I do know you need blood and I said how do you know that? They said because your lips are white! Then I told them I just dropped a lot of blood at home and I am about to faint. They rushed me back and started to do a work up on me and they soon told me that I was lucky not to of had a heart attack because if I did I would of died on the spot because by their records I dropped nine pints of blood at one time and the body only holds twelve. If I had a heart attack there would not be enough blood to get in my heart much less my brain. They were getting me ready for x-rays and a colonoscopy to see if they could find out why I had lost so much blood, I mean I had not injured myself so I couldn't imagine but only one thing, maybe its cancer. So, there I was butt naked getting prepped and I began to pray in my mind, Dear Lord Jesus, I don't know what they're going to find wrong with me but I am afraid they're going to open me up and find out I have cancer, please Lord hold my hand and say a prayer for me.

About that time, a tall black guy grabbed the top of the curtain to where I was in ICU, and pulled it back real hard. (Now mind you its 2:30 in the a.m., and no one knows I am in the emergency room), this guy was dressed in plain street clothes, and He said, Are you Terrie Broom? I said I am. He said," My name is Jeremy and I have come to hold your hand and pray for you!" I remember thinking as I was going out from the pain meds and anesthesia was, Jesus, I didn't mean literally!!! The thing I remember thou is I knew God heard my prayer in my heart that I was praying without a doubt. That really got my attention. The next day when I awoke I kept asking about this guy Jeremy but no one knew of him at all. I really think he was an Angel of God sent to speak to me and let me know he heard me calling out to him. Question now is will I hear him calling out to me? (YouTube-"there's nothing greater than Grace" Point of Grace)

CHAPTER FIVE

Weakness in Me

"I am not the sort of person that falls in and quickly out of love, but to you I gave my affections right from the start. I have a lover who loves me, how could I break such a heart, yet still you get my attention."

I have to be honest, my story is definitely a process and you can know if The Lord was calling me the devil was trying to keep me enticed and in bondage just like Pharaoh in Moses time. The enemy will not make it easy and let you just walk away.

I had a lot of free time on my hands and even though I was searching for spiritual truth it wasn't easy letting go and not giving into temptations. There was several brief encounters I had with my past some of my old flames came out of the woodwork and pursued me and I did get caught up in them for a while, I won't mention names because it's their story too and one I am sure they wouldn't want me to reveal at this time. But sufficient to say there was one person in particular that I really loved and respected in a time when I first got into the lifestyle and was being counseled thru my church to go to a "homosexual Anonymous" if you will permit me to describe it was just like that.

I didn't want to go but promised my counselor I would go once. Well I drove up to this church where the meetings took place, I parked. I got out and did a turnabout and got back in my car and said, no I can't do this. Started my car, put it in reverse, and backed out and then said what am I thinking, I did promise to go so I parked in another parking place, turned the car off, sat there and psych myself into getting out of the car. I finally made it to the door and this young blonde beautiful girl opened the door and extended her hand and welcomed me and asked me to come on in, she could see that I was alone and asked me if I was indeed alone or was I waiting on someone and I said well yes, I am alone, and she said well come sit by me and my husband and I will be your friend.

She made a real comfortable impression on me and we did end up becoming lifelong friends, but that is another story for another day. We lost contact for many many years. I always wondered what happened to that couple who befriended me and reached out to me when I felt such like an outsider.

For many years I tried to find her with no luck. I looked on line every now then to see if I could find her in the search engines. When Facebook became popular I tried to find her through that. Strange how all of a sudden I found her through Facebook by seeing first her husband on there. I realized it showed him in his profile he was single and my first thoughts were oh no she has died!

But I knew she had at least three children by then so I looked up her oldest knowing that surely if she was still alive she would be listed as a friend on his Facebook page. Sure enough, there she was, I will just call her name sue, to protect her identity here.

I sent Sue a friend request and shortly she responded by actually calling me. I had already warned Kayla about this because I didn't want her to feel threaten or jealous, which for the most part Kayla always trusted me and hardly ever got jealous. So when Sue called me we reconnected. We soon made plans to meet each other for lunch finding out we lived like only forty-five minutes from each other. I was so excited to see her for she was truly an amazing person in my life. I had missed her so much, her and her husband had moved off to pastor a Baptist church in Tennessee years ago.

Well to my surprise when I met her for lunch one of the first things she says to me is she wanted to ask me to forgive her for trying to "fix" me all those years ago. She then began to tell me her story of how her and husband had divorced over his compulsion and addictions to sex and that he was gay too, and if anyone ever wanted to not be gay it was her husband, every time he repented he would get Sue pregnant and then he would go right back into the gay affairs.

She then informed me that she had a nervous breakdown and developed an eating disorder called Anorexia. She came through all that became stable again and met someone and remarried and had a fourth child. She then said her life had changed a lot and that she had changed in a lot of beliefs, one, that gay people are what they are and that she even saw herself as a bi- sexual.

I was like taking all this new information in, I mean this is a woman who was a diehard Baptist who didn't smoke or cuss who I looked up to as a strong Christian, this was a lot to take in about my long lost friend that I had no idea that her life had turned out like this, and in the back of my mind I started having thoughts just flooding my mind, like…., great, she is bi-sexual and I had always had a thing for her for she was so pretty. I'm thinking just the time I am trying to pull life together she is letting her life fall apart.

I really tried hard, I actually stayed away for a whole year to keep from getting too personally involved.

In time, I did start to spend a lot of time on the phone and hearing of her troubles and her many health issues I felt almost obligated to get involve because of who she had been to me in the past. Besides, it had been a year now so maybe I could control my desires when I was around her.

Looking back I can see clearly how the enemy and my flesh did not want me to be free from sin. My affair with Sue started out innocently by just being there to help her through her divorce and her illness from chronic migraines which would debilitate her capacity to care for her children.

I would come over help clean and buy groceries and sometimes prepare meals for them. Then it got to be where she would be alone when the kids went to their fathers for a visit and be really sick that I would call my partner and ask if she minded if I stayed the night with her because she was so ill and by herself and I needed to watch her or even take her to the hospital at times. Sue was a mess and really not the same person that I had known years ago. But, still I felt like I owed her something and I was bent on repaying it.

In time she began to ask me if I was happy with my relationship with Kayla. She would prod and ask questions about our sex life. She even told me of her sex-capades with other men and women. I started to feel a pull toward her being drawn like a moth to a flame. Then it happened when I least expected it. One evening we were alone and just talking, then she did it, leaned right in and kissed me passionately.

I looked at her and said I thought you said you were not attracted to me and she let me know it was a woman's prerogative to change her mind if she wanted to. I should of walked away right then, but something snapped inside of me and I thought well I had always wanted to sleep with her, now is my chance. I said to her looking into her eyes, you know your opening Pandora's Box? Which she replied, I love Pandora. So I ended up spending the night and letting my emotions and my flesh get the best of me. You know if you play around the edge of a mudslide it's inevitable you will fall in it.

I don't know how it works but I wore guilt like a badge. Kayla could tell something was off with us and she would accuse me of getting more than emotionally involved with Sue, to the point she started wanting to come and check this person out and see how bad her situation really was. One time I had to take Sue to the hospital and Kayla came with me and Sue was very needy and constantly wanting to hold my hand and I suppose by my own actions were telling on me, Kayla was steaming as a jilted Lover, in which that is exactly what she was experiencing.

When we got Sue back home after a couple of days Kayla and I would have one serious conversation. I, on the one hand was having a talk to my own self too. I mean, what was I thinking of sleeping with Sue, she was a mess, a shell of a person, very sick and troubled.

Almost homeless, without any means and out of work helpless and I let her drag me away and entice me to get involve in an affair with her when I had someone at home who REALLY loved me and sacrificed a lot for me.

Something was telling me it wasn't Sue that was tempting me it was my own lust and desires and my own sin was pulling me in like a magnet.

I never admitted to the affair. I excused it. I made it look like I wanted it to look like and I decided I would pull back and make steps to get away from Sue, she was not good for me and I was not good for her.

CHAPTER SIX

I have decided to follow Jesus (old time Hymn)

That Summer I tried to really to work on my relationship with Kayla. I paid a lot more attention to her and celebrated her and her achievements. Life was getting back to normal.

We took a vacation to visit my Aunt and Uncles in Oklahoma. We went on long weekend trips things were getting better because we were paying more attention to each other.

We started going to church more on a regular basis, especially since our Mega church just opened a satellite church right about 3 blocks from our house. We started going to the Dream Center location and seeing some of our friends from an earlier small group we use to attend was very exciting and we enjoyed their company, these were two women that were in the closet about their homosexual relationship. We found ourselves in a small group of sorts that were closeted Homosexuals.

There was this one woman that was going there she always introduced herself to Kayla and me. Every time we came each week Beth would reach out to say hello by our name how she kept remembering us I thought was amazing, I mean did we stick out that much?

Well any how I kept running into Beth every time I turned around. I would see her at the grocery store, gas station, I mean she even came into where I was working at a restaurant and I finally said, listen Beth, it is crazy how we keep running into each other like this, and I mean it must be providential that we become friends. We both laughed, and she was glad that I would want to be her friend. She was letting me know she was starting a small group and wanted to invite Kayla and me. I said thanks, we been thinking about getting involved in one again. So I told her I would talk to Kayla and get back with her.

When we were at church the next Sunday I mentioned to our other friends about Beth, and told them they should come go with us. There was a small sect of gay people that were going to Highlands. It was easy to come and be a part of such a big church, you really didn't have to commit just come and go. No one has to know you and if someone does try to connect or build a bridge out to you all you have to do is go to another campus and stay there till it happens again. Most of our gay friends where "hoppers" they would hop from one campus to the next. I guess they just couldn't bring themselves to be transparent with anyone.

Well our friends decided to come and go with us to Beth's small group. It was great, we were just doing word studies over different words, like peace, comfort, joy, humility finding the definition and where they were found in the scriptures and how we might recognize or apply it in our circumstances and so forth.

I could tell how serious Beth was about studying, she had several different translations of the bible she was like old school with a concordance and dictionary as well; unlike the rest of us who had our cell phone apps and iPad apps and all this technical stuff, most of us didn't even use a bible but a bible app on our phones or iPads.

The small group was going well, at least far as I was concerned. One of the girls that was a friend of mine called me and wanted to know if Beth had called me and asked to go to lunch or dinner? I said yes actually a few times she has invited both Kayla and I to her house and out to eat. Well, my friend said, I find it strange that she would call and invite me out. I told her she was over reacting and that Beth was only trying to get to know her and I was sure she was making her rounds to everyone in the small group. My friend said there was something about her that did not sit well with her but she couldn't put her finger on it. She asked me if I thought she might be gay, since she had a roommate living with her. I thought that was ridiculous, not everyone who was single in their 50's and lived with a roommate was necessarily gay. I mean I didn't get that vibe at all. She seems so sold out to The Lord, and involved in the church and community I could not see her in that way.

We were going every week and I really enjoyed learning more and more and being prayed for on a weekly basis was bringing peace into my life. But for some, my friends that were gay and for Kayla they were feeling uncomfortable.

Kayla started making up work reasons why she could not come, that she really had to work late. I found out really that it was all because she felt so inferior to others in the group because she couldn't find the scriptures and she didn't know the stories in the bible enough to talk about it in a in depth conversations and she felt like a bump on a log so to speak that she didn't want to continue to go anymore.

Then, my gay friends started to tell me that I was becoming enamored with Beth that I was developing some kind of "Christian gay crush" on her, which I told them they were absurd to think such a thing. Yeah, I was attracted to Beth but it was so different.

I was loving how she was so devoted and in love with Jesus. I loved how she was involved in her community how she served and thought of others and would put others before herself. I saw how when she was unemployed by a layoff how God provided her a new job. I witnessed how she worshiped at church how genuine she was, it made a definite impression on me and also actually convicted me of how selfish and self- centered I was living. I began to think I don't even think I am a real Christian at all.

One Sunday, when we were worshiping and singing this song I had heard many times growing up, "I have decided to follow Jesus", the praise leader stopped in the middle of it and with the music playing low he began to tell us the true story of how that song had been written so many years ago.

The story goes back in the early 19th century there was a great revival in Whales, England. As a result of this, many missionaries came from England to northeast India to spread the Gospel. These missionaries came to some headhunter tribes which were aggressive and primitive to say the least.

One Welsh missionary finally succeeded in converting a man, his wife and two children. Angry, the village Chief summoned all the villagers. He then called for the family who had first converted, to renounce their faith in public or face execution. Moved by the Holy spirit the man replied," I have decided to follow Jesus. No turning back". Enraged at the refusal of the man, the Chief ordered his archers to arrow down the two children.

As the two boys lay twitching on the ground, the Chief asked, "Will you deny your faith? You have lost both your sons. You will lose your wife too." But the new convert replied again with tears in his eyes and seeing the tears in his wife's eyes saying," though none go with me, I still I will follow. No turning back."

The Chief was beside himself with anger and ordered his wife arrowed down in front of him. Now the Chief asked for the last time, "I will give you this last opportunity to deny your faith and live." In the face of death the man said," The cross before me, the world behind me. No turning back. No turning back. He was then shot down like the rest of his family.

Something then strange happened. The Chief who had ordered these deaths was moved by this man's faith. He wondered, "Why should this man, his wife and children die for a Man who lived in a faraway land on another continent some 2,000 years ago? There must be some supernatural power behind the family and I too want that supernatural power."

In a spontaneous confession of faith, he declared, "I too belong to Jesus Christ!" when the crowd heard this from the mouth of their Chief, the whole village accepted Christ as their Lord and Savior.

Now can I tell you there wasn't a dry eye in the church this Sunday, including mine. I was really moved by that story even thinking about how on the news just a few days ago it was reported how ISIS was executing people Christians mind you left and right and how Jihadist were making themselves to be suicide bombers all for a religion, a false god at that.

I was disturbed and convicted realizing that I at that moment could not honestly say I would or could lay down my life in believing in Jesus Christ.

I realized that I didn't think I was a Christian at all. So, I prayed, "Lord Jesus, I do not know you like that. Jesus, I want to know you like that! I want to be able to lay my life down for you should you call for it. I Lord, surrender all that I am not, and all that I am to you; come into my life forgive me and fill me with yourself and change me for your Kingdom I desire."

That was a most pivotal moment in my life and it's like Jesus came into the Temple of my heart and turned the money tables upside down.

So I got saved before church even got started that morning in the midst of worship. What way to get saved!

Later in the service the pastor was teaching about how we need to have someone that we could trust in our lives to confess our sins to and so that they could pray for us in doing so we could be healed.

"Confess your sins to one another, and pray for one another, so that you may be healed. The effective prayer of a righteous man can accomplish much." (James 5:16)

I thought about that more later on in the day and after we got home and finished lunch I just looked at Kayla and said, hey I am going to run over to see Beth for a minute I want to tell her something. I jumped in my van and drove the short distance to speak with Beth.

As I walked up to knock on the door Drenda, Beth's housemate answered me and said, "well hi Terrie", and I said, "hey do you think I could speak to Beth?" Drenda said, "Why sure, come on in Terrie" and she called out to Beth and I believe Drenda invited me on in and offered me something to drink and then Beth came into the room and I said, "I am sorry to pop in on you like this I was just wondering if I could share something with you." Beth was like, "well sure, I was just about to take a walk down the street, would you want to go with me and walk and talk?" I said, "Sure, I can do that."

So off we went and I started in by saying, "that was a great service today wasn't it?" Beth agreed with me and then I said, "well I hope that you don't take this as a weird thing but I feel like I want to adopt you like a sister. I mean I have watched you for months and I am drawn to you, not like in an attraction like I want to be with you in sexual way but I love you like a sister. I mean I love how you live your life, I have watch you study and depend on the Lord I see how you love people and sincerely pray and go out of your way for people and I have watch you worship God. Beth I want to live like that too."

"Today in the message when they were telling us we should have someone in our life that we could talk to and be able to trust and confess our sins and pray with so we could be healed, I thought of you."

Well, Beth just listened to all of that, and at first I think she was taken back from what I was saying, I was so hoping she would not think that I was coming on to her from my background trying to say I was attracted to her in a lustful way, I was just dying inside hoping that I had said the right thing, trusting the prompting of God.

Then Beth, slowly began to say, "Well Terrie, I have never had anyone who wanted to adopt me as a sister before, matter of fact I don't even have sister so that is awesome. I will tell you though, I am following Jesus. If you're attracted to anything in my life it's not me, it is Him."

"Another thing I want to share with you is you need to consider, if you're following Jesus get ready, he might just call you to do something in your life that you are not yet ready to do." At that moment I was not so sure what she was talking about.

I mean Beth had not once ever confronted me about being gay or being in a committed same sex relationship. But she did intentionally reach out to me time after time never putting me down but always taking an interest and always bringing Jesus into the conversation. I have never experienced anyone like that before.

Usually the Christians I had encountered were always judgmental. I do remember telling her that I felt like I was gay and I didn't know what to do about that in relation to Jesus. And I will never forget what Beth said, she said," just take one step at a time and He will lead you in to all truth". You do not have to make all decisions right now today, but listen and He will tell you the Truth and the Truth will lead you to do the right thing." Well we were now back in front of her house so I said I needed to get back home I just told Kayla I had to come by and see you for a minute, but before I left Beth said, well let's just pray and ask God to bless this and your new journey into following Him. That was typical Beth and I would find that out more and more as our friendship grew.

When I got back home it was like the atmosphere was put on pause and Kayla didn't even ask me why or what I did over at Beth's place. I really didn't even want to explain it either. I was not sure how she would perceive it and maybe she would respond like my other gay friends and say I was experiencing some kind of gay Christian crush. Only The Lord knows and knew my heart, but I really believed that something wonderful had changed in me I felt brand new clean and fresh.

I really believe I truly had surrendered my life unto Jesus and he came into my life. I mean what does John 1:12 say, "but as many as received Him, to them He gave the right to become children of God, even those who believe in His name." That is what I had done that day, I had received Jesus, and now I have the power and right to be God's child.

CHAPTER SEVEN

Jesus loves me

Now I had this new experience deep in my soul and didn't really know how to share it with anyone. I kept doing life as I had always done it, for me it had become so routine for my partner and I.

It was get up at the crack of dawn go to work come home feed the dogs take something out of the fridge prepare supper clean up, let the dogs out and then in again and crash in front of the t v until we fell asleep. The only real bright spots now was going to church and going to small group. Those had become "my" days and "my" time for myself that I longed for. Like I was saying by this time Kayla had quit coming to the small group and to church all together, so we were really starting to grow apart. I was continually recording Joseph Prince on the DVR and watching it in the evenings. Then my parents for Christmas gave me a NOOK which I got totally wrapped up in by watching Youtube videos of whatever was interesting to me about God. So looking back, it is true I did not pay near enough attention to Kayla, but I had always tried to share what I was reading or learning and she really never acted like she even cared or was interested in it, so as time went on I just introverted into listening and watching more and more on my tablet with my earphone plugs in my ears than talking to Kayla. This was now becoming a problem and a source of tension between her and I. she constantly complained about it and I would say it was no more different that her bringing a book to bed to read before going to sleep.

As time went along and I started studying the Bible it became more and more clear that God was showing me about relationships. God's perfect plan. How the red thin line throughout the book was all about Jesus God's own son. How he created a bride for Himself. The bible clearly talks about marriage. It never once describes or talks about any other marriage. In Heaven it's all about a Bride and Bridegroom. Its God's perfect and only plan. When I saw this and it sunk in I realized I had been duped.

I had been deceived. I had been lied to. I started praying and asking The Holy Spirit to teach me the truth and let me see clearly and it was like the scales on my eyes were falling off daily. I felt so perplexed because I did love Kayla and yet I was realizing more and more I had made a mistake and I was living in an opposed relationship that was totally out of God's design and will for mankind. I kept trying to use my human reasoning trying to build a case before God because some where I knew I had read in Isaiah it says, the Lord says come let us reason together… but I was trying to tell and explain to a Holy God that I had already made a covenant to Kayla before people I could not end our relationship!

Then I found in Corinthians where Paul says if your married to an unbeliever don't divorce in whatever situation you came to in the Lord you should remain. I had all these excuses that I thought God would let me stay with Kayla. After some time in prayer I heard The Lord say to my spirit… "My covenant supercedes any covenant that you could make. " Meaning my covenant meant nothing in His eyes. So with a deep conviction and enlightenment I told the Lord that if this was His plan for me to leave that he would have to do it, for I couldn't and didn't want to hurt anyone, and to be honest I didn't have anywhere to go, I didn't even have a great job to support myself. I had a flood of excuses going through my mind.

I just knew I had to surrender and lean not on my own understanding at this point I had to put Christ first in everything. I was so ready to leave everything for the gospel sake.

We started a new message series at church, it was on the four cups my Pastor Chris Hodges even wrote a book on this topic. I had only known of the one cup that was passed around at the Lord's last supper. But in Jewish customs the Passover actually had a ceremony within the Passover that they drank from four cups. These four cups that had wine in them represented four promises that God spoke to the Israelites and I believe still speaks to us as well today. I sat under Pastor Chris's teachings and the Holy Spirit would speak to me and tell me these same promises. One, God wants to free me from bondage, this slavery that I had been bound to and lied to had held me captive unable to free myself. Two, God wants to deliver me from whatever was holding me back, all the fear and unbelief and even rebellion. Three, God wants me to discover His original intention for my life, to know who I am in Christ, and that I fall under a new covenant of Truth and Grace it is God's intent for His Spirit to live in and through me doing His goodwill and fulfilling His purposes in and for me. Four, God wants me to be a part of a family that is making a difference in His Kingdom.

Each one of these promises was a journey for me and not easy. I felt more and more deeply in my soul that God was bringing me out of the gay lifestyle. I at times would want to grab and hold on to it for fear of losing everything. I would even buy sweet endearing cards and write long expressive desires and wishes for Kayla to read and be connected to me even though

I knew she was trying to figure me out; I know I must have been confusing to her at times. I would draw close to her but then feel pulled away at the same time. It was literally like a tug of war inside of me. I told the Lord again and again if you are calling me out of this you must make it happen. I have no one but YOU, where will I go and what will I do?

It was about 3 months and circumstances had come into play that Kayla decided I needed to have my own checking account. We had a joint account for over 13years, she had a savings account and owned stocks, we both shared a safety deposit, and I had life insurance policies. But with my health being bad she wanted me to try to get on disability and if I was going to apply for it I needed to have a separate bank account. So I did that. Then out of the blue, our van that I drove most of the time broke down and I had to get another car right away and for no reason really we decided to just put it in my name alone, usually we put our cars in both of our names but we didn't this time. By now we had moved and the house we had was actually in Kayla's father's name, he bought it out right for us and we were paying him back. So actually now all of a sudden the financial strings that were tying us together were coming undone right before my eyes. I had a thought in the back of my head as I realized this for the first time, "I could really walk away at any time", how can I do this?

I was pretty sure I could hear The Lord saying it's time to come away, I love you and I have called you to a new life and I do love Kayla too, I need you to get out of the way so I can save her. I have you and I will catch you and raise you with my righteous right hand. Trust Me. I want to bring you out of this darkness and the sin that so easily entangles you.

I waited for The Lord to go before me and to open the door, I was willing to go forward if it meant losing my best friend for my Savior, my better friend who loved me and died for me who then raised to life again and gave me a forever gift, His presence by His Spirit which lives, moves and has life manifesting through mine now.

It was June, Father's day weekend and all was beautiful including the weather. Kayla made plans to take the whole weekend off and we had a great time hanging out, going to Pepper Place (a great outside farmers market slash arts and crafts with some entertainment venue that she never gets to go to because it's on Saturday mornings from April to August each year) we really enjoyed the morning, then we decided to do a picnic at the park taking the dogs to the city park for a great time of walking and sitting in the sunshine, having a picnic. Then in the afternoon we took the dogs to the pet store to wash and bathe them taking pics one after another.

Then Sunday we met my folks for lunch to celebrate Father's Day with my immediate family and it was a great time. Later on that day Kayla got called into work for an issue she had to go and see about and problem solve. When she came back, as she walked in the door my whole world just shifted on a dime and it became a paradigm. She came back in a tyrant. She came in the door as I was again, watching Joseph Prince on t v, she started in on me and accused me of having an affair.

She came in and said "what's going on between us"? I was like, "what are you talking about"? She said, "who are you seeing, I feel like there is someone between us I just know you are having an affair"!

I looked at her and said," are you crazy? I come home every day, I am here cooking diner waiting on you to get home, I am DVR-ing Joseph Prince and listening to that, when do I have time to have an affair?!" Then as if I could actually feel the Holy

Spirit tap me on my shoulder, it hit me, I said, "you know what you're right, there is someone in between us." Kayla said, "okay, so let me sit down, you're going to be honest with me, good." I looked at Kayla and I said, the person that is coming between us is Jesus. Well that just lit her fuse! She exploded and jumped up and said, "You're kidding me, for real?" She stormed into the bedroom and slammed the door. I was sitting in my chair and just praying, I said here we go Lord. If this is it, if this is You opening the door to leave at this time help me NOW! If she pushes me I will take this as a sign that you want me to leave right now.

I surrender to what you are wanting in my life and I have to do this by faith and trust that it is you and not me. About then, Kayla came out of the room yelling and being very loud and dramatic waving her arms in the air and was asking me if I was gonna let this church come in between her and I. I told her I would wish that she would come and learn as I was learning that no one knows it all and she could gain so much insight by just absorbing information, but she would not agree to come and go with me. I finally said I can't drag a dead horse to drink water, I shouldn't have used that terminology, I meant to say I can't drag a horse to drink water....she never would let me live that statement down, calling her a dead horse. As she was going on and on I just felt the Holy Spirit say, "it's over".

So, with that in my Spirit, I said Kayla let's just call it quits.... it's over, we are done and I need to leave. This is where I am and it's no longer fair to you for us to keep living together; it is a lie.

She couldn't believe I was saying this. But I said it and I meant it. She asked me to please stay til atleast September. I said I would think about it, that I had to figure out what to do and where to go, but I couldn't make any promises.

Then there was silence. I just broke off a fifteen year relationship that was my whole world. But God, He moved me and called me out and from that moment started to bring me out of my darkness into His marvelous light. ("Jesus Loves Me" – Chris Tomlin).

CHAPTER EIGHT

Amazing Grace

It being June I was staying involved with a summer small group. I was still going to Beth's small group. Each time she was doing something different. This was a short summer session so she decided to do it on prayer. I was trying to play my guitar more and more and I felt like The Lord was leading me to bring the guitar to group and play it while we were praying. Our group this time started out small and even got smaller till after a couple of weeks it was just the two of us, Beth and I.

We looked at it as God's will and His divine providence. It really offered me a time to listen and learn from some wisdom that Beth had gained in her Christian life and it enable me to step out and open up and be able to confide more and more to someone who would actively pray for The Lord's will into my life. I had told her of how I believed The Lord was asking me to step out in dynamic faith and trust Him that I believed He wanted me to leave Kayla and leave the gay life. Beth would ask me tough questions and challenge me to make some next steps. I am grateful that she was there to keep me accountable. I think Beth was my first real friend, she had the marks of a true friend, she accepted me as I am and she would encourage me and sharpen me with the word of God as iron sharpens iron. Beth would also acknowledge my journey and when I was feeling down and having to lean in and trust in The Lord, she would very often remind me of how far I had come and how much I had grown in the trusting of The Lord.

Beth traveled from time to time and she was great to offer me a chance to earn extra money by dog sitting or house sitting. The week that I broke up with Kayla, I was to house sit at Beth's. In the midst of Kayla carrying on and going off on me about why I would leave her, and how could I do that and all the things I suppose someone would ask and beg your attention about, my cell phone rang and it was Beth and since I was to house sit for her I felt like it could be important so I answered it and I was right, Beth just wanted to tell me some logistics and what her plans were, the days she needed me or didn't need me and when she would leave and arrive back.

In the midst of this conversation Kayla was breaking picture frames crying and yelling at me while I was on the phone. I was trying to tell her to stop and she shouldn't be breaking all these frames with glass because our pets, three schnauzers, Romeo and Casper and Lillie could step on this. Beth could hear all the commotion and emotion and she was like, "gee Terrie if you need to come over here earlier and land for a minute know your welcome to do so". I said," Thanks, I think she will calm down but I will keep that offer in mind and I appreciate it very much". Well we finished our conversation, and when I got off the phone things just got worse instead of better. I did not get any sleep that night, I was glad it was Friday night because I was off for the weekend.

Kayla was breaking pictures of us and tearing things up and it ran through my mind that I had better get some things that meant a lot to me and put them in a safe place, like my car. So things that were mementos of my Brother who had died, things that were special to me I started packing up in the car.

When I came back in the house I didn't realize how much of my belongings were like "mementos". There was this look that looked like some things were missing here. Then I just heard The Holy Spirit say, "You need to just pack it all up and leave". So I started taking everything I thought was mine and or fair to take.

I felt like she was getting the house and property, she was keeping all the dogs and she had the best car and she had she had she had, I decided I was going to take what money that was in the safe deposit box at our bank. It was six thousand dollars. I felt that it was fair. Well, here I am I have left my lover like one of those fifty ways you do it …..Slip out the back Jack or drop off the key Lee, and get yourself free.

Now this is where if you think the enemy is going to give you a free pass and let you just walk out of Egypt without a struggle you need to keep on dreaming of those leeks they were eating back in Egypt.

It's like if The Lord gives you a word it will be tested. So here I have my whole car packed down and I realize at this moment I am truly homeless. So I drive over to Beth and Drenda's house to see if I could use some of her basement space to store what I did have and take her up on that landing pad till I could figure out my next step.

Drenda was like I think you need to talk to Beth first it is her house and she has just left to drive out of town, but you knew that because your house sitting for us. Drenda said well just call her and ask her about it so I did. I called Beth and told her the situation how things had gotten worse and out of hand and I felt like I should leave now. Then Beth is like well, wait I am out of town, Drenda is having some family over for the weekend give me till I get back into town Sunday for us to sit down and talk about it. I was like okay. Well here I am with all my belongings in one car and I truly do look homeless. Okay God where to now?

So I am needing a place till the weekend is over I know God is just testing me if I will follow his lead and not just run back when the first thing doesn't work out. I calmly prayed, "Lord you said you were calling me out. I took the step, I packed my things that I could and now I need to know what to do now"?

I sat in my car and a thought occurred to me I should call my friend Sallie and ask if I could stay with her. So I called her, the phone rang and who answered was not Sallie or Terry her husband but an old mutual friend of ours, Rhonda. I said, "Hey Rhonda! How are you and is Sallie there?" She informed me that Sallie and Terry were on vacation in Disney World, and she was staying there for a little while. I was like "great, well I need to come over and crash too!"

Rhonda was like you need to call her and make sure that is okay and all. (I thought why wouldn't it be okay I am like a member of the family with her) but I agreed to call her, and so here I go calling Sallie while she was on vacation, I just knew I would probably catch her riding that "Magic Mountain" rollercoaster, but as it would be she answered and was at a place she could talk with me and I told her the news how I had really broken up with Kayla and she offered her condolences and asked me how I was and I told how I was homeless, that's how I was. I told her about how Beth had offered me a place to land for a minute but now as it was she too was out of town and had some guest staying at her place, which I would have to wait till Sunday evening to talk to her before I could do anything. I see Rhonda Is out at your place and she wouldn't let me come over without your permission, I just need a couch and a shower for two days, would it be alright to hang out at your place this weekend? Sallie was like of course you can stay. So thank God

He worked that out, the next stop would have been under the viaduct (VI dock)!

I was able to crash on the couch for two nights and then Sunday evening I met with Beth. First off she wanted to know all that transpired and I told her. Then she said she wanted to pray for me and Kayla before she told me what she had on her mind. So she did. She praised The Lord in her prayer that He was doing what He loves to do for those who will surrender and be still to follow after Him. He takes his righteous right hand and brings his children out of the dark and into His light. She prayed I would stay sensitive to His calling and follow after the voice of the Holy Spirit and not a stranger and I remember her praying for Kayla too, to be open to hear His voice and to receive His salvation as well as I had just recently. I was so grateful how Beth had always treated us always so kind and patient never judging us just praying God would speak to us.

Well, after that she had a notepad and she laid out what she felt was in both of our best interests would be.

She said right away you need to look for a better job, working part time would not be enough to sustain me, which she was right. I needed to get up every morning like I was going to an 8-5 job, if I was working that day fine but when I got off at noon I needed to start applying for jobs. I would have to also let her see my finances and she would teach me how to make a budget and live by it, that was her forte, she exceled in teaching finances and how to organize and budget incomes. I would need to keep every receipt of every dollar I spent, that once a week probably on Sunday nights we would go over it, reason one, she said she didn't want me to be living it up when I needed to be preparing to move on. She felt like three months would be adequate to me staying there and if by the end of October I hadn't found an apartment we would just re-visit this time frame. I needed to pay her fifty dollars a week for rent and I could use anything in the house that I needed. If I could not comply with any of what she just said I would not be able to stay there.

I thought all she said was fair, the boundaries were clear and only right so I agreed to the conditions and accepted her offer and then I moved in. I basically had the whole downstairs which was very gracious of Beth. I had a bedroom a den, the laundry room was very accessible and my own private bathroom with a shower. Everything I could need.

This transition was all providential, The Lord knows just what and who we need in our lives. Even thou it was difficult to leave Kayla it was also like I had the power of Grace for it. I had such a novacaine experience I was numb to the feelings and was just doing what I had been told to do by the Spirit of God. Without His Grace I am sure I would not have followed through with it.

The Lord is good to provide me with a place to land, to get my heart right with Him, and to use Beth to teach me how to budget my income and to pray and to encourage me to take the next steps to follow the Lord's will.

The next day July 3rd, I got up and got dressed and started to look for a new job, full time and with benefits. I went down about a mile from Beth's house and felt like the Lord was leading me to apply at Pep Boys which is an automobile service store, with my experience I should qualify for the job.

I walked in and asked for the manager and the guy told me he is right here but he is on the phone he will be off in a moment. So I stood around and just looked the place over I could hear him talking on the phone, he could see me and we smiled at each other. He was quite attractive, and later he introduced himself to me as John Cruse, not to be confused with Tom Cruise. I told him my name was Terrie Broom not to be confused with Terry Mop....we just both laugh. Then he asked me what brought me in and I said underemployment. I am looking for a full time job.

He smiled and asked about my experience and many other questions and he seemed to like what he was hearing and told me to go online and apply for a service writer position on their website and to mark I was interested in that location. He warned me it was pretty lengthy application so he also said to call him right when I finished so he could look at it.

The next day I got called in for an interview and usually it takes weeks of interviews but it "just so happened" nothing I believe just happens it is the way the Lord works for all things work together for those who are called to His purposes; anyway that his supervisor was in town and he (John) would interview me and then his Boss, Randy would interview me the same day probably at the same time over lunch. He told me to come by the store by 11:30 and he would see me then.

So I arrived there and I met Randy and Randy was like come on John, let's go to lunch and talk to Terrie. We went to a Mexican restaurant that was close by and we got us some lunch and Randy started to talk and he asked me of my experience which totaled about 18 years of automobile experience from selling cars to being a service advisor my last five years. He after talking a lot about the Pep Boys Company said if I wanted the job it was mine. So yes I want the job and when can I begin!! So he said next week. That is how it happened just like that. I got a full time job the first day out looking, now that was The Lord!!

I had the fourth of July off and it felt good to just relax and breathe. Then I realized it was and would have been my 15 year anniversary with Kayla. I can't lie, that was a long tough emotional day but I just took my heavy heart and told the Lord He would have to carry this because it was too heavy. Then no doubt the heaviness just lifted off of me and it was like that novacaine again, I was able to rest and not feel the pain of a broken relationship, I knew it in my mind but my soul could not feel the pain.

The summer was great! Beth and Drenda both were being a light for me, spending time talking and walking in the evenings and sharing God's word learning to listen for the heartbeat of God.

I fasted a lot; it was soon our churches annual 21 days of fasting and praying. We did it corporately those who could would meet every morning at 6:00 am for one hour til 7:00 am or for those like me we just rolled out of bed at five til the hour and got online to listen to the devotional and worship music and prayed in our pajamas and afterward got ready to leave for the work day. I fasted tv, all soft drinks, I ate a lot of salads too. I decided to flood my mind with listening to worship songs form like Hillsong and used my nook to continue to watch my favorite preachers. It was important to keep hearing the word so my faith would be strong especially if I started listening to my human worldly reasoning.

The three months were coming to an end, the summer faded away fast, and I had agreed to move out from Beth's place by October 31. Beth kept encouraging me like she did when I was looking for the full time job, I was spending my off days looking at apartments, sometimes 4 at a time praying God would go before me and find the perfect place to be my own little place of an oasis.

The first week of October came and after listening to a lot of advice from a lot of people pointing out places I could live and checking them our finding that either they were too expensive or so terrible on the inside, I just knew I needed something quick the end of the month would be here before I knew it. I got alone I just spent time praying and declaring that I would find the perfect place.

I told The Lord, He knew me better than I did so please open a place for me to go and live that would be safe and nice and an oasis. When I was at work, it seemed that I was being asked to go work at a different store every week. That got old, but I prayed first for things to settle for me and for me to have a permanent lasting place so I could find a place convenient to fit my needs and activities.

I went in an asked my manager if I could get a permanent store to work at and they sent me to a place in Homewood. I drove around the job area and there were several apartments on that side of town. I passed this one place and The Holy Spirit said go there.

I went in to the manager's office and inquired about one bedroom apartment, and they informed me they had brand new studio apartments that were spacious and the building was all new. They were not letting people move in till next week and they had a great special. Well for starters only the studio apartments came with the power, water, cable, trash pick- up included in the rent. Furthermore the special is 300.00 off your first month's rent, 200.00 off second and 100.00 off third month's rent. The rent was only 670.00 a month with a 500.00 deposit. They took me to see it and it was beautiful all new appliances, microwave, oven, fridge new ceiling fans and a balcony with a screen doors that weren't broken.

It was all so brand new I felt like THIS IS IT!!! And it was. I filled out the credit application and was really worried that I might not get approved, it hadn't crossed my mind till then. I struggled for days waiting to hear back thinking what if I didn't have good enough credit, my income had grossly declined over the years. I asked Beth and others to pray for my need of getting my own place and that it would be the place that God would want me to be. Well, after a week I got a call and I got approved.

Which worked out I didn't have to get the power in my name nor cable so no more extra deposits required. It felt like it was all falling into place. I had a great sense of peace over it.

As I was driving back to Beth's place to tell her all about it I was listening to the radio and the Christian artist Chris Thomlin's song came on," Amazing Grace my chains are gone".

I felt that song go right over on me and through me and to me. It was so true in my experience. And little did I know how much more amazing my life would be to me in the months to come. I was sensing my chains were definitely broken and I was a captive set free and redeemable. I knew I had a long way to go and grow, it just felt so right being in the middle of God's will in my life, I could finally know what true rest was like.

CHAPTER NINE

Just be my Father

Beth and Drenda was really excited for me that I was able to get a lease on an apartment, maybe they were sweating it that I might ask them to be a co-signer.

Beth and I went on our evening walk to walk the dog but mostly the walk was more for Beth to walk off stress from the work day. While we were walking Beth discussed with me what my next steps might be. It was soon to be the fall and winter semester for our church small groups to re-start again. She encouraged me by just re-telling me of how far I had come and how much I had grown from that one day, by using faith to trust The Lord and to decide to follow Jesus. I had went through the Church's Growth Track, I had joined the Church. My next step was to stretch myself and go to a life group. At this point I had been going to Beth's small groups, but this time she was teaching on finances and budgeting on Godly principles and I had learned a little of all that during the summer months staying with her. I told her I think your right and I think I am ready. Life group, then was called,"Living in freedom everyday". It was a group usually divided into gender groups unless it was one for married couples. It was a twelve week meeting where you got to know people and dealt with personal issues but even more, it was a study that took you back to where Sin originated and learning the differences between the Tree of Life and the Tree of the knowledge of Good and Evil. It has always been about a choice and even is to this day we all come to a place from making a choice from which tree we will eat from today.

My first notes from that group give you a hint to where my heart was:

> *Every day we face opportunity to make choices. Yes or no, will I or wont I. The choice I must make is, will I choose to be still and give the Holy Spirit His way; to allow the Holy Spirit to make clear His direction for me so I can truly choose life?*

> *The right choice. I can start right now today by stopping and waiting on His move, His voice and trusting him with obedience. Not what's easy for me or what is obvious, the true way is trusting His direction for me-- not everyone else's.*

I was excited to go to this life group, there were many different ladies from different walks of life. There were older ones, business leaders, career adults and young single and young married with children and then me, the one gay girl.

No one for weeks on end would really open up and share. The leaders wanted to pray over each and every one of us each week so we could get use to the retreat that was to happen at the end of the semester. At the retreat there would be a lot of praying apparently.

I knew eventually I would need to open up to my leaders and share where I was in my new walk with the Lord and I was just waiting for the opportunity to do so. One evening when the group time was over I knew we would be getting prayed for so I dashed off to the restroom first.

By the time I came out every single person had left and apparently didn't want prayer that night. So with a deep breath I felt this must be the moment to be open with my core life group leaders, Chris and Nancy.

So I told them how this was my next step, I had recently surrendered my life to Jesus Christ and walked out of a fifteen year relationship and out of the gay lifestyle, trusting the Lord because He Called me out.

I told them of how all these things had transpired, all the things God was doing and providing and how I wanted to open up here in this group but felt like no one wanted to be that open for this group was really quiet. Well I could tell by Nancy's tears and Chris's deep intent eyes they were moved by my story and man can those two pray! They covered me with prayer and protection and blessings they covered it all. I left there that evening knowing that I was in the right group and God knows when to open the time up for one to share.

In the middle of the next week I got a call from Nancy one of the life group leaders and she said she wanted me to call someone who might be helpful with me in my journey to wholeness. At first I thought, their pushing me away and off on to someone else. Also, I had felt a little rejected from Beth recently she was just so busy and she was leading a small group and she hadn't been really available for the last couple of weeks. Now here I am and these leaders of mine wanted me to call a perfect stranger to help me out! Well Nancy told me to write this number down and give her a call. So I did write the number down but I struggled for like two weeks in wanting to call and tell another person about my life. I mean I had shared with Beth and Drenda, my campus Pastor, and the life group leaders I was like I am all shared out. I had a terrible experience with a counselor twenty years ago and it put a bad taste in my mouth to be willing to go through that again was hard for me.

When Sunday came I went to church saw my friend Beth and she invited me over for lunch and a chance to catch up. That made me feel better. We caught up on life and things she asked me how it was going with the new place and how did I like my new small group. That's when I just wanted to get her opinion on this contacting this counselor that Nancy was recommending.

Surprisingly Beth was encouraged for me to think that they would take the time and effort to find an asset for me to use. I was like, gee Wally I didn't think about it like that. I was like also, well, what am I supposed to do just call up a stranger and just introduce myself and tell her what?

So at group the next time I saw Chris and Nancy afterwards when again everyone left without prayers, they asked me if I had called the counselor; I in turned ask them did they want me to leave the group, was I to much? And to my relief, they were like goodness no!! Not at all, they told me I was so welcomed there but they felt like I needed a little extra guidance that's all. Nancy said, "look Terrie, we have never had to deal with homosexuality in our group before and we are not sure how to best serve you, we want you to have the best experience in this process that you can have since you have now stepped out of in faith." Nancy encouraged me telling me that the counselor, whose name I will keep out for she wants to keep her anonymity, was a former lesbian like myself and had been out of the lifestyle for over fifteen years and was a dedicated Christian and that her parents went to our church, but she herself went to another church where she was starting a ministry to help people just like me. Then Nancy said," just call her, she probably wouldn't even answer the phone, she works another job as well as being in the ministry, chances are she won't be home". Okay, fine. So as I was driving home from group that night I decided to call her from my cell phone on my way home, and guess what? You got it, she answered on the second ring!

I introduced myself and said you don't me but I was told you were expecting my call. I told Her a little bit of who I was and where I was coming from. I told her I wasn't really expecting you to answer the phone I was just wanting to leave my name and number. She suggested that we should meet and talk in person and go from there. So we set up a time after church to meet at a local coffee shop to talk.

After I got off the phone I was really having second thoughts of starting with another counselor, so many memories of how my last experience sent me over the edge. I just got through forgiving the last counselor I had for interfering with my friend and roommate in 1993.

When Sunday came around I was to meet Her at O'Henry's a local coffee shop. I sat there and thought, well this is good, after all that talking we didn't discuss how we would recognize each other. So sitting there, I with every patron coming in the door I wondered is that her? Wouldn't you know it when you stop looking they would come in the door and then stare at you wondering if that's you? So finally we locked eyes on each other and I guess we both just knew and at the same time she said Terrie? I said her name, We both smiled and said yes.

I had already gotten a table and wouldn't you know it, the place was really crowded, mostly because it was drizzling rain and all the outside furniture was wet, forcing most folks to sit inside or take their drinks and go. I was feeling a lot of anxiety of talking about my life out in public for fear someone might know me and hear me talk. Yes that would be paranoia setting in. Luckily

The Counselor did most of the talking and encouraging. She gave me a DVD of a guy who I had never heard of before, Ricky C. She asked me to look it over and see what I thought about it.

She gave me a something like a questionnaire to fill out along with a release form saying I understood that this was a layman program through the church, that they were not psychiatrists nor medical doctors that it was a ministry to help those who wanted to grow in their spirituality and seeking sound doctrinal wisdom. That I would agree to give them the right if at any time I felt suicidal to turn me over to a medical attention. I thought wow this is heavy...but I could see it being necessary as well.

After coffee and talking she gave me that DVD to watch and the counseling forms to fill out and we set up another time to meet at her church office.

When I got home I watched the DVD. Never in my life had I ever heard my life explained so well. This guy pretty much told me how I grew up and the challenges that I had went thru and the psychology behind it as well.

I was quite intrigued with it all. I could see how my identity had been stolen from me at an early Age.

My true identity was stolen from me before I was born, my mother dearly wanted her firstborn child to be a boy. She has often told me she wished on many a red bird cardinals during her pregnancy that I would be a boy. In listening to this guy's own experience it opened up my eyes further to see how Satan tried to plant seeds all my life through my parents, through word curses, through society who would think just because I loved the color blue or climbed trees or could out run the boys or just because I wanted a motorcycle I should have been a boy.

I often struggled with identity issues. I always felt like one of the guys in my thinking and in my emotions. I even remember overhearing a neighbor one time tell my mom that her kids were screwed up." Terrie should have been a boy and Tom should have been born a girl." The truth is my brother and I were never brought up right, we never had been affirmed in our gender. Meaning my parents didn't have a close relationship with us and they were clueless to our needs.

The first time I met this Counselor at the church for our first counseling session I felt so nervous and felt such apprehension. Nevertheless, I was eager to take the steps to see how The Lord might use this to help me grow. When I walked in and I found The Counselor

walking toward me and she was smiling and saying "Hi, how are Ya?" She has this infectious laugh that can just bring a smile on your face. She was trying to find the key to one of the offices down in the basement of the church. She asked Joy the church secretary if she knew where the key was, I asked where the restroom was while they were hunting down the key, I was still thinking, should I stay or should I go. I could still back out, but no. I had come this far, I had filled out the questionnaire and I was wanting to go forward not shrink back.

When I came out from the restroom they had found the key to the office and we were making our way to it, and She asked me if I was able to finish the forms she gave me and what did I think about it. I said, " oh yeah I finished them and I found that the questions brought up lot of memories of what you do and don't like about your parents, and there is too much to jot down on that little line there. She was like good, well let's just pray first and she did.

She prayed to the Father asking Him to come and be with us here that He would give us wisdom and insight. And with that being said with the in Jesus's name and Amen, the first question came at me like this. "So, um, what would you say is your biggest issue today is? I said, "well, um, I feel like I am a project to some of my friends, well the few friends that I have. I began to tell her about being in this small group called "LIFE", and how I felt like I am the only person that is stepping out and I don't feel like I can really put anything even out there because nobody in the group is really wanting to deal with anything. I mean some of these people it's their second or third time going through this, I mean you knew what you were signing up for, I kind of had an idea about what I was getting into because I was warned that you're going to get in there learn about the origin of sin see how it affects your life and everyone's life and your gonna work thru learning how to forgive those who have offended you.

I mean you can't even serve on the "Serve Team" at the church until you have gone through this small group event. I really wanted to be involved in the church in some capacity. But anyway I was saying I am in this group and no one is sharing or dealing with anything. I end up staying behind every week just so I can share with the Co-leaders it's the only time I can share because no one is willing to put anything out there.

That's why I feel like a project, I am here because I've been told to come here to see you, because it's my next step and Its almost like a "push off", I mean, I really ... I think to be honest....I am not going to say, I am not attracted to some people, but uh my small group leader that I had before (this life group I am now in) who has really been a friend for me, to help me come out of all this, not that she told me to come out of this lifestyle, because I really did make the decision to walk out of it,(as I was sitting there spilling my guts to this Counselor, she just intently listened, and I had this fog come over my mind that I couldn't even remember how it was that I had come to make a decision to leave my lover of fifteen years.) I mean on what conscience level did I just up root my whole life and leave?

I was telling the Counselor that I felt I had so much oppression and depression on me in the last week that I can't even remember why I left! I knew it had a lot to do with the season, it's the holidays coming up Thanksgiving, the anniversary of my brother's death, two days ago it was my partner's birthday, Christmas coming up a lot of depression and anxiety realizing I wasn't going to be with Kayla and her family for the first time was in the back of my thoughts as well. Then I had gotten a call from our Veterinarian, wanting to change an appointment and push it back a few hours, I didn't even know that something had happen to one of my pets, I had to call Kayla and deliver that message and deal with that; and let her change the records to not call me in case of an emergency anymore because she was not going to let me have the decision making privileges from now on. It was upsetting that she would not let me raise at least one out of the three dogs.

I mean I am just bouncing off from one thought to another out loud, I mean I'm looking back and it's a wonder she didn't go find me a straight jacket right then and there! Then on top of all that I change gears again getting back to the "issue today" of me feeling like a project, I was saying about my first small group leader, that I am really, I mean I am drawn to her, and in my heart I know it's because of her life, because she lives for Jesus. That's really the attraction that I have. And the Counselor agreed shaking her head and saying yes. Then I go on to say," But of course the enemy wants to take this Godly relationship and twist it and turn it into something that it's not. I am praying and standing against it, and all my friends are saying, you're just infatuated and enamored with this small group leader because she is a Christian, and you want both a woman and woman who is a Christian too, but it will all wear off." Then the Counselor asked, "Now are these your gay friends?" and I said, "yes." Then She told me some good news and advice.

She let me know that was something she struggled with as well, "coming out of the lesbian lifestyle how do you relate to all these women who don't have any of these attractions; and the enemy would just torture me", she said, "you know like I felt like I was walking on eggshells if I did this or if I said this you know what I mean?" And I had to agree I had felt like that too.

But she then told me that I could know that if a woman is in leadership, God has protection for that, and He is taking care of it, that you can trust Him that he has already worked these things out in these women's lives. And that's what you're attracted to, you want that same thing. And that is not wrong to want to be like that, to be strong in your spirit and to have everything you need in Christ to be confident in who you are.

That's a good thing to want. Then, The Counselor said, "and so your friends who are still living in this life are going to continually be speaking things that are not true, and those are distractions from the enemy to try to get you confused and get you to feel unbalanced, and then guess what; you are going to give in, do you hear what I'm saying?"

" So, your counsel and the things that your struggling with you need to take that stuff to believers and not share that kind of stuff with them (my gay friends) because it's gonna cause you to be way more confused. I know this is where you've always gone to, and these people know you and its more comfortable, but what you have to realize is that the people you are going to for counsel within the body of Christ, they have got God as the head and their hearing from Him and so the wisdom is coming this way, (as she demonstrates with vertical actions with her hands up and down). And if you're getting advice from nonbelievers it coming this way (illustrating horizontal actions, left to right), if it's not the wisdom of The Lord, what does the scripture say? It's demonic and we can't trust it. Alright?"

She told me to not just take people's word for truth to live by but to take every piece of advice or words of knowledge to prayer and ask the Holy Spirit to confirm and bear witness to my spirit. She told me to take even the things she tells me to take it to The Lord and let Him reveal the truth in any matter.

So, that is where we teeter, we try to stay in between those two worlds, and the Lord wants a time where we are set apart, nothing but a one on one where we are established in Him, where we have that wisdom, we know what is sounds like we know what it feels like, we know who we are. Then, we can be a witness to the world because we have been called to be Holy as he is Holy.

Holy, the word holy means to be set apart for use. So, there is a time period, when you think about the Israelites when the priest were chosen they had to go through a process, a time of purifying so that they could come before the Lord their God. It's the same with us. We have to come away from the world for a time. To be cleansed and purified and let Him establish who we are. We cling to this and stay within these boundaries for a while. Until our character becomes more like Christ.

At this time in my life I had thought I had done a lot of this coming away, I mean the whole summer I fasted a lot of things in my life I actually felt as if I was on a 90 day program for addictions. I gave up soda I fasted from TV, I only listened to worship music and I ate a lot of salads, but okay, that's because I was living with Beth and Drenda. But now I have moved on and I had started to realize I am really on my own, and when I was living at Beth's place there was such a peace I could really feel. But now that I am by myself I have begun to sense a different atmosphere and all of sudden I have a lot of thoughts and chatter going on in my mind that I didn't have when I was living in Beth's house.

The Counselor helped me realize that it takes time to develop a relationship. She gave me an illustration about how people train to identify counterfeit money, they stare and study and touch the real deal all the time so that when they see the counterfeit, they know whether it's real or not. That's what I am to do. We have to come away and get to know Jesus, we got to study Him seek Him and find Him. We have to cultivate a deep relationship with him and allow the Holy Spirit to teach us and reveal all truth to us so that we know and recognize error when we see it or hear it. That's where we want to be, so sensitive that we can hear and know truth or know what is false.

We have spent most of our lives living in the flesh, giving into fleshly ways, gratifying our flesh, that now we have to come to know and understand and believe the truth that Jesus died for us, now we want to come to Him and set our life apart for Him, we come away and separate from the world for a while and learn how to live by the Spirit not giving in to temptations, but renewing our mind with His word that's how we learn to know Him and then we can know Him well.

Before we can be a leader or step out into any ministry we must be established in Him, we come to hear and know His voice so we don't get out in the world and become confused in hearing other voices or opinions that distract us and cause us to wander off the path of life. It's His word that is a lamp unto our feet and a light to our path. If we don't get established in who we are in Christ the enemy will try to destroy us in our weak places. Our character needs to be developed in Christ.

We talked a lot that first time, the most important thing I got out of it was to realize what was coming out of my heart was the biggest tale-tale sign of where my walk with The Lord is and it will be expressed by my actions and words to those who I encounter alongside me. Now that I have decided to follow Jesus, I am getting rid of the bad influences in my life, getting away from the distractions that steal me away from His presence, getting rid of the sin, and I am no longer actively sinning now. I mean I am like a toddler who is wanting to walk and run but like in life you got to learn to crawl before you are walking. God has a grace period for that, I mean you wouldn't go up to a toddler and spank him because he couldn't walk a mile. No you just encourage him to walk a little more every day and as he grows up he can walk further and further.

We talked for over two hours that day I was amazed that she spent that much time listening but even more telling me that I was going to be able to become stable. God just doesn't zap us and we're okay and perfect. It is a process, I may fall down by learning to walk but I will not fall away, I am the Lord's I have surrendered to Him I have become part of His family. I am learning to walk and I may make some mistakes, but that's what God's grace is about, He enables me by his power to get up and face my temptations and learn to overcome the flesh by a lifestyle of surrendering my will, my way, what I want to what He wants.

He wants to establish us and transform us from our false belief systems. It takes time to learn and come into a right understanding of who God is. I need to start paying attention to what is coming out of my heart and where there is anger and rage or bitterness I need to acknowledge it and ask God to teach me His way, so I can start learning what love peace and kindness is; by knowing His Spirit and allowing His Spirit to live and speak truth through me.

He wants to heal our wounds that life has hit us with, let's learn His way by coming to Him and he will be in us giving us the ability to respond in a righteous and loving way. My response will be one of truth and grace that is found in Jesus.

The Counselor also loaded me down with lots of resources of books and devotional book to start giving me something to do for renewing my mind and encouraging my heart. Before we ended the session she had to ask me about that questionnaire I filled out she handed it to me to look at and I said," I don't need to look at it I know what I wrote in it, it's my life". She asked me if I wanted any prayer for anything, I am sure I did because even thou I am a new believer I had tried for many years to forgive my folks for being so immature and uneducated when it came to raising children or making a home for all of us. I was really still bent with bitterness that I couldn't even pray for them that day even thou I wanted to. We needed to deal with this another time. I couldn't do it at this time I felt like there was a barrier for sure.

It was about a week later at my life small group we were studying "Lessons from a river" reading from Ezekiel 47:1-12, this was a vision God gave the prophet Ezekiel it explained how there were stages to a relationship with God. There's ankle deep, knee deep, waist deep and over our head go with the flow deep. All of us when we become born again start this ankle deep position, but hopefully we can come to trust the presence of God and desire more of Him that we will want to go deeper and deeper to where we are fully surrendered to the "river" controlling us rather than us controlling our walk in and out of the river. This study had an impact on me because it reminded me of something that I had experienced as a child.

When I met with my Counselor later that week I told her about when I was about the age of 5 or 6 I was at the lake with my family and I was standing on the pier, and everyone was in the river laughing and swimming. My father yelled up to me to jump off the pier into his arms and I was like "no!" My father was asking me to jump into his arms and all I could see was the river and I could not swim. He kept telling me he would catch me and to jump, that I had better jump and with self-doubt and fear kept saying "no!" But my father kept persisting on me to jump that his tone changed I felt I had no choice I better jump, so I decided to trust him because he said he would catch me, so I ran and jumped off the Pier and it's like slow motion in my mind, but as I am in the air jumping toward my father's open arms which failed me because on purpose my father stepped back and allowed me to fall into the river which freaked me out! I sunk like a rock to the bottom and struggled to get back to the top of the water so I could catch my breath. My father eventually reached me and pulled me out but in my little heart it was too late, I told myself, "I will never do that again!" "That", meaning trust my father, he lied to me and I couldn't trust him. The Counselor stopped me in telling her this story and helped me to see that as a child I made an inner vow to myself against my father and also in the way I would come to understand God as my Father.

See I started to realize I had deep trust issues with my earthly father that effected my relationship with God as my Father. I had always accepted God as God, God as my Jesus my savior, but I never until this moment realized I needed to believe and receive God as my Father. Looking over the past several months I started to see my Father's arms and hands in my life. My Counselor explained how Father God is the protector, provider and affirmer of who I am. I mean here I am many, many years later and my Father God wants to redeem me from a childhood wound in my soul. I look back and see in my mind's eye how I was on that pier again, and God —my Father now was asking me to "jump", leave out of my fifteen year relationship that I loved, to TRUST in Him and that He would catch me. That is exactly what I had done, I believe God gave me the faith to walk in His obedience and His call. I see now I jumped with no expectations except that he would catch me and HE DID! I see God's hand in providing me a refuge to stay under Godly protection covered in prayer and encouragement, watching God as my Father provide a place for me to live.

My Counselor taught me that God's perfect plan was for us to be a family, and the family is God's own design and was a blue print if you will of how He wanted us to come to know and believe in Him. God the creator of all, it is He, our Father, the Holy Spirit is like unto our Mother, she teaches and comforts and answers our questions as all Moms do; and Jesus along with being our Savior is also our kinsman redeemer, brother, our friend and companion. Hearing this opened my eyes to see, yes this is good and holy. The purpose of the family is to detach from the earthly and grow to cling to the supernatural spiritual family of God.

When I came home later that day I meditated on all that we talked about wrote it in my journal and I marveled at how the Holy Spirit brought up a wound from so long ago to show me how He wanted to heal and redeem my issues of trusting. I grabbed my guitar and started to worship The Lord and God my Father, it reminded me of this song I use to know from a child, and I played it and in His presence I felt it all come to a place of peace for me.

JUST BE MY FATHER

(Song written by Mary Ann Crumm)

I come to you so very lonely, asking that only that I

might feel your touch. Sometimes I wonder if

your there, I wonder if you care, I need to know

how much. Sometimes you are my Savior,

sometimes you are my Friend, but right now

Just be my Father and hold me till this darkness leaves.

I come to you tired of living and tired of giving and so alone. It seems that no one understands me,

I can't take what this life hands me,

Can't make it on my own. Like a child I come to you, not sure what to do or where to go.

Ever so gently dry my tears and calm my fears til I can come home.

Sometimes you are my Savior, sometimes you are my friend, But right now just be my father, and hold me til this darkness ends.

CHAPTER TEN

Oceans where my feet may fail

Here it is already December, it has been six months into this new journey. The small group "LIFE" has just ended with its "life retreat". I was glad to see my small group finally opened up at the end and I was able to definitely make some new friends. During this season in my life I am looking to see God as my Father and praying God would show up and reveal to me and express His love as a Father to me.

Christmas is coming around the corner, it is going to be so different this year. I had planned to be absent from this holiday –but God had other plans.

First of all I had been asking the Lord for a sign, one that would show me that I was on the right path and I was indeed in His perfect will. Here it is Christmas Eve and Brenda one of the women in my small group came by my work place and gave me an unexpected Christmas gift. I was so taken back and very grateful. I decided to save it and put it under my "Charlie Brown" Christmas tree so I would have something to open on Christmas day. When I got home that evening, the Holy Spirit prompted me to go ahead and open Brenda's gift. It was such a little box that I first thought well maybe it's a gift certificate to a restaurant or something like that and I could use it to get dinner. So I opened it and to my amazement it was a beautiful bracelet of a silver cross with gold and silver beads threaded with a leather string. There's my sign! The Holy Spirit started to immediately explain the meaning of the sign. The bracelet just spoke out to me with a message from my Father God. Looking at the silver cross it had a hammered look to it, silver which symbolizes redemption, the hammered effect spoke of it being worked into my life, the twenty gold beads symbolized all the past years I had been in unholy relationships that God had forgiven me for as it speaks of how He now sees me as righteous, and the four silver beads stood for the four redeemed friends that prayed and carried me to Jesus constantly. The leather band that held it together was reminding me of my flesh and how it could be pulled in and out at times. What a wonderful reminder of the Father's love for me, the cross of Christ is being worked into my life!

Another time God spoke to me through a painting of mine, I have had it for years it is an abstract painting. One night the Holy Spirit started telling me to look deep in the painting and to see something new I had never noticed before. He revealed Himself to me as Mighty God who holds the world back for me, and He showed me He was always there looking over me when I was young. He showed Himself on the cross and his hand nailed and bleeding. I saw within that painting His head bowed praying for me. It is here I know God is answering my prayers for a sign, He sees He knows and He is ever present with me and through different ways keeps telling me the message "I will never leave you nor forsake you". The Lord is truly watching over me and looking to provide what I need. I can feel His presence with me.

My niece just called me on my cell phone to ask me to be at my parents for Christmas day. I wasn't going to go but I felt pressured to be there if anything to keep the peace. So now I have to go out on Christmas Eve night and buy Christmas presents because you just can't show up empty handed, not with my family. I prayed about it and I felt the Lord just told me to be generous, for I know that is how my heavenly Father is in His giving. So I headed out in a thunderstorm to do Christmas shopping and get it all done before the next morning.

First I had no clue what my family needed or wanted— but God does! I bought things that the Holy Spirit told me to… and most of it was on sale! One of the things I bought was for my mother, a nice outfit she is always complaining of never having anything to wear. Lo and behold wouldn't you believe it when she opened it she was thrilled. It was one of her favorite designer's and even my brother Tom had turned her on to this designer years and years ago and I had no idea about it. I got my little brother a pair of really nice slippers that he just raved about, and almost bought them for himself but wanted to wait til after the holidays so he could possibly get them on sale. Everyone loved all their gifts and I believe it's because I listen to the prompting of the Holy Spirit.

That evening my Counselor called and wanted to invite me to her parent's house to eat Christmas dinner. When she first invited me I didn't know what to say. I believe she worried about me being alone on this holiday for the first time. I had nothing better to do than stare at the four walls in my studio apartment so I agreed to come over. It was a lovely evening eating with Her family. Her mother was so nice and her father too, welcoming me in to share the holiday. After dinner we sat around and talked and they told me all kind of stories about their family and family mischievousness that were hilarious and at times had me in tears for laughing so hard. Then, I had assumed they had already exchanged gifts but no they hadn't, which I felt awkward. They had went out of their way to give me gifts! I was so surprised a lot of the things they gave me were practical for my everyday living for my apartment I was still getting settled in to it. Stuff for the kitchen, gift card to a favorite grocery store, a plunger…who'd ever thought I would need one but I didn't own one! A lot of little things that when you don't have it, it means something to you, something as little as a can opener it all made me feel special. Turned out to be a wonderful holiday thanks to my friends and family.

December 29th, 2014 this day's reading in the devotional of "Jesus is calling" spoke of trusting Jesus with every fiber of your being. That was a big issue with me. I am just now learning I can trust Father God to love me, protect me and be my provider. It starts with tiny steps through daily life experiences, as we are stretched and encouraged to take dynamic steps of faith. You see I did it backwards. I jumped off the cliff of a mountain and now I am looking for the angels to come and save me, lest I strike my foot up on a stone or commit emotional suicide!!

God has not left me, His Spirit is in me, His light is arising on me and His purposes are being developed in me with my daily journey through His promise land. As this year is closing out with 2014, I am so looking forward to the New Year to see and discover all that will come from my time and presence of the Lord in my life.

I am encouraged by those who God has chosen to speak life to me. I am grateful for their time, words and testimonies of how God has proven His love in their experiences within their struggles to live a surrendered life unto The Lord.

New Year's Day my Counselor sent me and some others this email to encourage our walk with the Lord.

If Abba Father's heart were hard or disproving toward us, we might be justified making other people, places, things and events our priorities, blazing a trail through life. But our God is the One who controls the times and seasons He is Lord overall and by His grace and gift of saving faith He has come near to us through Christ Jesus with love in His heart and healing in His wings.

He is never in a hurry, yet He is never late and always on time. He is God and He is ours! So we can trust Him, seeking always to stay sensitive and fully surrendered to Him.

We can ask Him at the start of each day, yes at the start of each year to direct our path and to order our steps, to show us when an interruption is really an opportunity, and to protect us when the enemy seeks to destroy.

Let us pray then with the Psalmist David, "make me to know you ways, O Lord, teach me your paths and lead me in your truth and teach me, for you are the God of my salvation; For you I wait all day long" Ps.24:4-5.

Let us be reminded to" keep our hearts with all diligence, for out of it flows the issues of life." Proverbs 4:23.

And to walk in His Spirit and not gratify the desires of the flesh. To be kind compassionate and forgiving in all our relationships. So the world may know us by the love that abounds in our hearts towards Him and others.

Ephesians 4:32

Then at the end of our lives, along with the Lord Jesus, We will be able to say to our Father, "I glorified you on the earth having accomplished the work you gave me to do". John 17:4

Then at the end of the e-mail She wrote out us a prayer she was praying for all of us.

It read as follows:

"My prayer for you is that you awake tomorrow to start a New Year with an increased sense of God's presence leading you nearer to the heart who is said to "rejoice over you with gladness and exult over you with loud singing" (Zephania3:17)"Gracious Father, on the eve of this New Year, we ask that you would make our hearts ever more sensitive and surrendered to your Spirit.

Make your love increase and abound in our hearts toward you and others. May we know you, follow you and glorify you every day that you give us on this earth and then for all eternity in your presence. Through Christ Jesus our Lord, Amen!"

During this season my praise song that was my favorite to get lost in was Oceans, by Hillsong United. Look it up on YouTube and you can listen too.

Chapter Eleven

Lord I am ready now

Here it is January 2015! A new year and once again The Lord has whispered to me a new word. He says this is the year of Trusting Me. At first I was excited to hear this word and declaration from The Lord, then I had second thoughts immediately, this must mean I will be in some tight spots if I am going to have to trust The Lord. Then, I heard this verse and I received it as my own promise from God.

Psalms 71:20; Thou you have made me see troubles, many bitter you will restore my life again; from the depths of the earth you again bring me up.

So much going on now with the holidays behind me and so grateful for the Grace that carried me through. I have been spending my free time reading, reading and reading. My Counselor loaded me down with books and I am truly a slow reader. But this one book meant a lot to me it is called, "The heart of the problem". It helped me to see and recognize that what I say is a reflection of what is truly in my heart and therefore exposes me sometimes unknowingly.

If I am acting out in fits of rage I have a big anger issue in my heart. Scripture tell us to guard our heart for out of it flow the very issues of life. If I will listen to myself I can help myself and see my sin and repent and confess my sin to The Lord, then He is faithful to cleanse me of all unrighteousness.

If we keep things inside that are harmful, like fear or anger the enemy can use it to shipwreck our faith. The Lord loves us enough to press us when the time is right so that the thing He can see in our heart that is not of Him will be forced out, not to harm us or embarrass us, but so that He can take it out of our heart and replace it with something of Him. Scripture states that the heart is deceitful above all things, and desperately wicked; who can know it. (Jer. 17:9)

Well God knows our heart totally. We should be about knowing His. The Lord himself says He will Himself will take out our heart of stone and replace it with a heart of flesh, one that is tender toward him. He allows some painful circumstances to get it up and out, it isn't meant for evil, or harm, but for good and healing so we can go on with life and be successful.

He loves us and has a wonderful plans for our life. I love the fact that Jesus wants and desires us to belong to him in a relationship and not just join a religion. It's a walk, one step at a time. He knows the end from the beginning, we only see the past and the present, that's why we must trust Him and know He is a good, good Father no matter what.

This is the time of year our church corporately fasts for 21 days. A lot of people say they want to hear God. But do they really? I know for a long time I dodged church because I was afraid I would hear God and then have to make a choice.

The chatter of the world and all the background noise and what you call "white noise" is all too much distracting you can barely at times hear your own self think. We as born again Christians have to come away from the things of this world to hear his voice.

If you turn off the TV and the radio and get out of the magazines and worldly novels and get in the word, The Bible and pray and actually be still, you might hear Him whisper your next steps toward a direction you would of never of considered. Thy Word is a lamp unto my feet and a light unto my path. I am learning this is true more and more. So I asked The Holy Spirit to take me to the Word of God each day to lead me to a specific verse or passage that He would like for me to meditate on and I am going to write it down to look back on for encouragement.

The first verse that The Holy Spirit led me to has really become my life verse, especially from where I've been saved by His Grace. It's 2Corinthians 4:2 (amp) We have renounced disgraceful ways (secret thoughts, feelings, desires and underhandedness, the methods and arts that men hide through shame);we refuse to deal craftily (to practice trickery and cunning) or to adulterate to handle dishonestly the Word of God, but we state the truth openly (clearly and candidly). And so we commend ourselves in the sight and presence of God to every man's conscience.

This Word of God became alive to me in my spirit, it means and lives to speak to me that I have made a decision to turn away from a lie to put away the sin and disgraceful way I was living outside of the will of my Father, and I was no longer going to manipulate the scriptures to justify my rights to a way of life that was so contrary to my Fathers perfect plan. I have been called to believe the Truth and to know His word is life and the Word draws me to His way instead of my way. If we really would get honest with our souls and stay and lay in prayer and seek the The Lord, His Spirit will lead us into all Truth and when we believe the Truth it will cause us to live in Truth. Then our true identity will come forth easily and honestly, we are the children of God and if truly children of God we will not continue in a life of habitually sinning but a life of freedom living in the power of Grace and Truth. Our security and sanctification lies in the Person of Jesus Christ through His Holy Spirit who lives to teach us and comfort us and bring us in to all knowledge of His divine and extravagant love for us.

When I took my dynamic step of faith, trusting myself to at that time blind faith, to leave my longtime lover, I left with what would fit in my car, I had no furniture not much of anything besides a TV and my clothes a few mementos of my brother Tom and some gifts. I have watched as God my father who knows my needs has gone before me and provided at the right time just what I have needed. My parents and I have slowly been able to re-connect, we both see how we have failed each other, me with forgiveness and them with realizing how poorly they had been a productive and affirming parent. My parents were very kind to me to help me with some dishes, and when I lost my car key while at work they came to my call and helped me pay for a locksmith to cut me a key and allowed me to pay them back whenever I was able to do so.

Then when I was sick and missed several days of work they assisted me in helping pay my rent which in the past they would of never of done. Then, I have been blessed by the Body of Christ, people unknown to me helped and provided me some furniture a nice futon not a cheap one either a rather comfortable stable piece of furniture that met a great need for me.

When my ex-partner cut me off of our shared medical insurance I had to get my own through my new job, when I got it and I went to pick up my prescription for insulin with insurance my cost for one month's prescription was one Thousand dollars! I quickly said I can't get this! I mean I was only making one thousand dollars a month as it was. I recall saying three things are gonna happen, one, The Lord will heal me, or two I would be going into a coma eventually or three, God would provide my medication for me! As I walked out of that drugstore I had these thoughts from my heart: Lord You are my hiding place whenever I feel alone you surround me with songs of deliverance, I will trust in you, let the weak say I am strong, let the poor say I am rich. Thank you Father for providing all that I need that pertains to life and holiness.

I got a text out of the blue from my friend Drenda, it was so encouraging to hear the words of confirmation. She texted me this:

"Prayed for you this evening, these are the scriptures I felt I was supposed to agree

With you on, Psalms 34: 15, He hears our cry; Romans 8:15, receive the spirit of adoption,

Matthew 16:19, He has given us the key to the Kingdom of heaven, to bind and to loose.

I pray and bind up discouragement and release joy, I bind up disappointment and fear has to leave and to be replaced by peace and boldness with clarity along with a sound mind are yours!

Confusion cannot stay where the presence of God is.

Hoping you're doing ok."

My friend Drenda did not know what I had just been through but the Holy Spirit did. And The Lord worked through Drenda and brought me to her heart and she prayed for me this day and then reached out to text me with a word of encouragement and specific scripture to speak to me and The Lord used this to strengthen my faith. He heard my inward cry of fear and discouragement and disappointment. Not knowing my situation Drenda that week when I was over visiting Beth gave me some insulin that she had extra she was very kind to give it to me it was enough for a month….just what I needed, thank you Father!

It's Super Bowl Sunday, my thoughts and feelings led me down a path of remembrance. This would be a fun memory for me how I would usually be setting up the weekend especially Sunday when I would for Kayla go to the bakery and get a super bowl cake and balloons and decorate a little and share in her excitement for the Super Bowl. I actually felt a little homesick, took me down a road from one thought to another I do miss her, but I have to reclaim my focus for my mind back to where I have surrendered and submitted my life unto Jesus, He is the center of it all. My happiest days with Kayla does not surpass my most difficult day with The Lord, He is my Door of Hope, my faithful Father whom I am putting my trust and security with. I got on with my morning and went to church and worship was amazing and refreshing just what I needed.

We have to be careful, sober and alert at all times in our minds, for the enemy is like a lion roaring seeking out who he can devour. 1 Peter 5:8; All the enemy can do is roar, we have to depend on the voice of the Holy Spirit to dismantle the lies of the roar. Jesus is our shield and the word of God is our sword, when dressed in the whole battle armor we are protected and then we can stand firm on the ground established in truth, grace and in His protection. Let me just say, the enemy will come in so subtle if it is not through a thought, a good memory or even a friend, how faithful are the wounds of a friend, right? I have had to learn and re-learn time after time to take EVERY thought captive to surrender it to the obedience of Christ knowing I trust him to show me if it's good and fruitful or trash.

Later on in the day my Counselor called to invite me to their church that evening because they had a guest speaker who was a singing prophet. She encouraged me to replace old memories with new ones so the enemy couldn't play with my emotions of the past. There was truth in what she was teaching me. So on a whim I said okay, if you meet me there I will come and listen to this singing prophet. His name is Scott Windam, he and his wife Shannon allow the Lord to move within them to sing and prophesy the Word of the Lord through him playing the guitar and singing and speaking over people, and yes he called me out, I was one of the few that the Lord chose to let me know I am exactly where I need to be at this time. He is taking the pain away, and I will be able to run again and not be weary. Then he sang a song over me how he will restore all that was lost or eaten up from the locust…how he will never leave me or forsake me. This was truly a blessing for me to be singled out to be loved on by the Spirit of God. The song in this season of my life is from PLUMB," I am ready now". Check it out on YouTube.

Lord I am ready now…

Chapter Twelve

I am not who I was

Today was along day even longer night, thirty-two hours.... I can't sleep. Been reading the book "Agape Road", by Bob Mumford. Reading this book I am realizing the "hook" that he is talking about of self (eros) love has been deep in my life. The purpose of my life is to Glorify The Lord in all I do and all I say. It is not what I can get or manipulate for my benefit. Love is not like that, God is love and he does not act like that. I remember reading for the first time how God announce just who He is unto Moses, He said as He passed by Moses in the cleft of the rock," The Lord, The Lord! A God merciful and gracious, slow to anger, and abundant in loving-kindness and truth, keeping mercy and lovingkindness for thousands, forgiving iniquity and transgression and sin." (Ex. 34:6-7). What a great God we have who is patient and longsuffering not wishing that any of us should perish, but that we would come to know Christ and to be known by Him.

I know how blessed I am. If it were not for the many prayers of my friends and family I may have suffered more in this life by never coming to the knowledge of who Jesus is. Self- love had me bound up deep within my life. I have been having a lot of dreams reminding me how twisted my thinking can be and revealing more soul-ties. When I was at the retreat for my

Life small group one of the exercises they had us do was to take a 3x5 card and write down any of our known soul ties. I remember chuckling, thinking I was going to need a 8x11 sheet of paper for this. Well, what they would do with that is pray with us over each person we had entered into an unholy relationship with through emotional ties or sexual ties and ask the Lord to break and free us from any tie that bound us to that person or even thing.

I decided the more I thought about it, I really wanted to be free from any distractions or ties and I really want to be free to move on. I made a list to deal with once and for all. I am so thankful for God helping me see the error of my ways and to come to the saving knowledge of Jesus. Thank you Lord for each person you have used to help me keep my eyes continually on you. I got with my Counselor and asked if we could meet at the church and to pray through these many soul ties I had and let's specifically break them off and away from me one by one. I even asked Beth to come and be in agreement with us and to be my witness. I by my faith in Christ chose to close many doors that I had opened to walk in disobedience of foolishness and rebellion. I asked the Lord to sever all soul ties that were holding me back and to return all that was mine to me and to let go and send back all that belonged to the other person and to heal my mind and the depths of my soul. I had the Counselor there to guide in the process with prayer, and Beth as my sister in the Lord as my witness. I know who I am in Christ and from this day forward I will submit all that I am, and all that I am not to the purposes of The Kingdom of God. I have renounced all lies about security, love, acceptance, provisions, and protection and reclaimed the Truth. The Lord revealed to me that I am surrounded by His love, my identity is in HIM. I have liberty to live in freedom and without fear and doubt. I know now what and who is Love. Love is specific, not controlling, never keeping a record, long suffering and patient, kind and generous. 1cor.13 tell us what and how love performs.

Jesus is the Door of Hope, He opens the door to eternal life that no man can close and Christ closes the door on my past that no one can open! I am past the threshold into His presence, I am able to stand by His Grace and by His blood that cleanses me entirely.

I was accepted from the foundations of the earth, He has always been here and there in my past in my present. He the Lord hovers over me with His wings and arms of salvation, His light overshadows me from all darkness, He is my rear and front guard. He will not let anything come against me that will not first come through Him. He is my shield, He fights my battles and sends His waring Angels to defend and protect me. I am going to trust Him to protect me. I can and will shift the responsibility to His shoulders. I hold this resolution to know I am not to be judged but to see I am accepted in the Beloved family of God. I am learning that I am a reflector of His Light, I don't have to hide, and I can let God my Father filter goodness and shelter me from any harm. I can love and say I love you in an innocent and with a pure motive, it will not be turned against me. I am Holy and blameless. I am like David fighting Goliath, one stone strong and my giant is dead!

Its been over a week since I broke off all those soul ties; it must of worked for they have come out of the woodwork to try to re-connect! People I haven't seen for years, people I haven't talked to in months and now that I have cut the ties to my loving dogs even Kayla all of a sudden is calling and now wants me to help her out and be there for the dogs. This is not strange nor does it catch me off guard. These soul ties will not always just let go they will try to reconnect through all kinds of ways, with texting, calling, and through mutual friendships. They will begin to wear on your soul again trying to make you trust in your flesh and then leading to sin again. I am now aware of the schemes of the enemy. I have set my heart and mind to the purpose of trusting God. The enemy lies are being uncovered daily. I must speak the Truth and embrace His correction. Lord live in me to do your goodwill in this life.

I thank God for the Body of Christ and the Spirit filled believers you have blessed me with. To have someone I can call on late at night that will pray and to counsel with me, they have encouraged me to realize that the Father has done his part in braking off all these soul ties from my past, now I must walk and do my part completely by cutting it all off in the natural. Not to reopen the door by cultivating old habits with people who are not walking in the light but wanting to influence me back to a life of self- love, self- motivation, self- deception a place that pulls me away from the way of right living and right thinking.

I recognized today that for years I had a belief system that was a lie. I could use Grace as an excuse to do and get or take what I wanted. I operated in a spirit of arrogance not confidence. I repent and I do recognize and see the lie; Father God, take this way of believing and living away from me. Let me live as unto You, by submitting my way and my will to Yours! I, understanding now, that Grace is a person Jesus, and He is the power that gives me the ability not to sin. Lord I receive your Spirit of grace and truth to lead me and guide me and to work to do your will and purpose through my life, to glorify you as you glorified the Father; so I want to do the same. Thank you for revealing this to me and cleansing me from all the wrong thinking and letting me experience who true Grace is!

The last few weeks has been a faith walk for me. While at bible study the question was asked, "what do you do when don't get your way?" My heart was revealing –sin, I sin when I don't get my way.

So many times I get mad and irritated that my way and plans or ideas get changed. I have recognized the interruptions and inconveniences of my time have been a barrier to my connecting to The Lord. I have had to learn the hard way through experiences that if and when I don't get to connect with a friend for whatever reason, I have to recognize that my times are indeed in my loving Father's hands. He may be calling me away to spend time with Him or possibly it is not about me, put possibly the friend who is needed to be somewhere else doing the Father's will at that given time. That is why it is so necessary to be in consistent fellowship with the Spirit of God, so we understand and can sense His leading us in our daily lives, then we have peace and joy and contentment as well. It is also a way of trusting and coming to know I am not going to miss out on one good thing that my Father wants and desires for me to enjoy.

I remember being so upset when a good friend invited me to spend a Saturday with her and then canceling the invite at the last minute, it wasn't about how the plans had changed as it was just looking forward to hanging out with someone on my day off. It's like it had happened for the up tenth time and I am disappointed once again. I heard someone say one time it's not money, it's not communication that breaks down relationships, its disappointment that destroys relationships. Just what is disappointment? It really is the feeling of sadness that is caused by the nonfulfillment of one's hopes or expectations. When we set our hopes and desires on friends, family or acquaintances we are setting ourselves up for rejection and disappointment. This has happened all my life to me. I allowed offenses to crack and open a door to my soul and then that was an open door for the enemy to have a right to attack me. That offense of disappointment and rejection set me up to be hurt and angry as well. The very act of resentment became a stumbling block and barrier to my connection with The Lord.

Once I came to the understanding that I should forgive and release the offenders in my life, and to ask Father God to pour out His love and peace to fill me I was then able to set my affections and desires and all that hope on Jesus. I came to know that he would never disappointment me for He knows all the days of my life and knows what I need and when I need it. Romans 10:11 says, "For the scripture says "whoever believes in HIM will not be disappointed." The enemy will use the slightest splinter of the flesh to create an infection in your soul to pull your eyes off The Lord and distract you from your purpose in this life. I see my purpose is to be a reflector of His magnificence and majestic light. I have to and need to position myself to receive His light in and to and through me for the people in my world to see. The way to do this is to get into His presence find the secret place and worship Him there and then be still and know He is God. I Thank Jesus for calling my name and loving me! He is in the process of conforming me to His image, I am His purpose and He is mine.

CHAPTER THIRTEEN

I will follow you

March 28th, 2015 Saturday; it has been a weak week, been sick and dizzy and passing blood...AGAIN. I am not wanting to go the doctor or ER. Went into work today, it is an amazing beautiful day the air is crisp and clean the sun is shining and warm. After being there for like thirty minutes I heard the Lord say to my spirit "it's time". I said to myself, "Time for what?" The Spirit said, "It's time for you to leave". "Leave?" I thought. "How can I just leave, I don't even have a job to go to?" And there, I am telling The Lord like He doesn't already know, I have to have a job to leave a job...I mean I got bills. I must have walked around that store for another hour going is this me or is this God? I knew this voice and this prompting for it is the same voice that said, "Trust me".

This is the same voice that said," I want you to come out of this darkness and the sin that so easily entangles you." So, I felt the Lord was releasing me from this job and I needed to again step out with this dynamic faith and leave. I went up to my manager and told him I appreciated the opportunity here but I needed to leave, and leave right now. He looked puzzled, so I said, "I am resigning-quitting my job". So off I left and to be honest when I surrendered all my worry and fear and asked for

His provision I felt nothing but peace as I left out the door of that place.

Even thou I felt peace, my body was still feeling sick. I didn't want to go the hospital so for like days I just rested hoping it would go away. By Tuesday I gave in and decided to go to the clinic my church owned; I heard if you were a member you would be able to get some assistance, I had insurance but the deductible under the Obamacare was so expensive I couldn't afford to be sick, so I de cided to try to go and see if I could get some help through my church's clinic they had with doctors who worked liked it's a mission. I was mostly concerned about my blood pressure so I asked if the nurse could just check my blood pressure and she said, if I check you and we find that you need medical attention will you go to the ER. I told the nurse I really couldn't afford to go to the ER but if I had to I would. She took me back and my blood pressure was okay, then she took a blood sample for some test and she said she would call me tomorrow.

My small group this spring was at Beth's house again and we were studying a book that one of her friends and Mentor had written. The title is "Things revealed belong to us", the title came from scripture in Deuteronomy 29:29. It's about Paige Jackson and her journey and experience of believing and standing on the promises of God and how we should speak and declare the promises over our own situations and circumstances.

While this was our spring small group it was a short six week study. Beth had decided to take one of our Tuesdays off reason being, one, it was in the middle of Spring Break and also she had to go out of town on a business trip. I was one of a few singles and we decided on our own to at least meet and get together to eat and fellowship. Even though I had been feeling terrible I wanted to keep my promise of meeting up with my friends.

So I got to the restaurant early and was standing around waiting on my group and I heard a familiar voice saying Hey Terrie! It was Joseph, he is one of the managers there and I use to wait on him when I worked at Panera Bread, which was one block down the street. He was one of my regulars. I smiled at him and said Hey Joseph. He asked me where had I gone and what have I been up to lately.

I said, "Well, I left Panera and went to work at Pep Boys and as of last Saturday I am unemployed and looking for another job". I told him of how I thought I was leaving Panera for a better opportunity and it did not work out.

He looked at me and asked, "Would you consider working for me?" I thought about it and said a prayer under my breath, well Lord if this is where you want me, open the door. I had in my heart been really wanting a Monday thru Friday and forty hours schedule so I could be free to do some photography work and be more involved within my Church on the weekends. So I said, "Well Joseph would you think I could have forty hours a week and a Monday thru Friday schedule and a certain wage"? He smiled and said, "I think we could work with those parameters, and he said, look I know you and I have seen you work and you have always from my perspective been very good and customer service oriented and that's what I need here". So he went to go get me an application to fill out and when he returned I told him I was meeting some girls from my small group from church and I would take the application home and bring it back the next day.

So wouldn't you know it the next morning about eight o'clock the Dr. called and said I needed to go to the ER right away for my blood count was dangerously low. I felt sick, now I felt very sick. Just happened my friend Sallie called me and I told her what was going on and I didn't think I could make it to the ER, Sallie was on her cell phone and was on her way to pick up her grandchildren to take to school and she was wanting to call 911 for me but I was like no, I will find a way, she lived too far off to help me so she told me to hold on and she called another old friend of ours Laveda to see if she could do anything, just happened that Laveda was with a new friend of theirs that was a nurse and Laveda called me and wanted to know what was going on, I hadn't really talked with her for years, and I had told her I was now a diabetic and not a good one at that and I had been off my medication because it cost way more than I could afford, I mean one month's prescription was as much as my earnings I made for one month and I just decided to not take it, I needed The Lord to make a way for me someway somehow. She advised me to call this county agency for medical assistance because I would probably be approved by my income situation. I told her I was going to call my friend Wendy who is a retired nurse and maybe she could come and take me to the hospital. I mean I still had memories when I was a teenager of doing odd jobs for Laveda and this one time I was at her house with our friend Sallie and I had a terrible ear ache, and Laveda said, I got something for that and she went and got some ear drops and I was lying on the couch with a bad ear infection, and I heard Laveda say, I need to warm it first, and I didn't think nothing of that, and Sallie didn't either, but what we didn't realize is she was warming it up not by the warm tap water but by using the micro wave oven! Needless to say when she came in and put the drops in my ear the liquid drops was a sizzling and boiling in my ear drum, I mean I jumped off that couch like a lunatic and said every cuss and foul word I had ever heard and then made up some too!

While I sit here now about to pass out on the phone I was like I really don't want Laveda to help me, but isn't is strange how The Holy Spirit orchestrates situations for us to heal us of the things from our past that has wounded our souls.

It is by no coincidence that I got to talk to Laveda and tell her about some of the changes God was doing in my life and how He had come to me and rescued me out of my darkness and how now I have decided to follow Him no matter what, tho none go with me. I realized that God is healing my soul one dramatic memory after another. I was able to forgive and release Laveda for hurting me and injuring me, looking back I am glad she did it to me and not to one of her small toddlers at the time, they could have been extremely injured.

Laveda did find me a medical assistance program called Needy Meds, it's a federal program for people in my situation. I am Thankful that Wendy was indeed available and able to come and get me and take me into the ER. I am also thankful for each of my friends who prayed for me daily. The doctor did an upper and lower GI tests to find my bleeding concerns and the news came back I have Diverticulosis, by now the bleeding had stopped and they gave me a blood transfusion and now I am back to normal. I've got to stay on my medicine.

Through this experience I have learned to rest, trust and rely on the Body of Christ. The Lord brought people from my past that I had forgotten about and opened the door for me to forgive and release them from my anger, disappointment and the bitter thoughts I had toward them. The efforts and lengths the Holy Spirit will go to for me to be drawn out of the pain and darkness is so incredibly redeeming and freeing.

I was in the hospital for about 4 days and I was released. I still have no job. I asked Beth if she would call and explain to Joseph why I hadn't come back by with my application like I told him I would. He was very impressed by the where for all to call and follow up and to inform him of what had happened that I was in the hospital. I wanted him to know I really was interested in working for him. I called right after getting out of the hospital and we set up an interview with the other managers. I asked the Lord to lead me and guide me to the right place and opportunity for I needed a job quickly.

I was beginning to see that I really needed to trust in the Lord with everything in my life. At one point I was so distraught to think that the Lord was wanting everything in my life, every nickel and penny for I was going through my savings like sand in my hand. I had to realize that he wanted me to surrender everything and anything. He really wanted it all.

The Holy Spirit was healing my wounded soul and was bringing me to make new memories to replace old memories. It was coming up to April and Easter was April 5th, that was the anniversary of Kayla and mines first date that we always celebrated, we had went to Six Flags over Georgia on Easter.

This year I had been planning to get baptized soon, when the weather was warm, so I thought about what my counselor had said that God would in time bring new memories to replace the old ones. So I contacted my campus pastor and told him I wanted to be baptized on Easter since it was on the first Sunday of the month when our church did baptisms I thought what would be a better time than on Easter to commit my life in an outward demonstration of the new life I had received.

My pastor has often said that baptism is the wedding band of Christianity and after sharing with my close friends and small group I had a little wedding party of my very own to be my witnesses. I was so excited that the Lord was redeeming me from my past.

I have this thing for numbers, and the number "five" is the number of Grace. I was being baptized on April 5th. I had my new friends and old ones there to cheer me on and after changing out of my wet clothes I was invited to my Counselor's family dinner for Easter and as we were walking out my Counselor handed me this envelope it was a card she said one of her elders at her own church had given this to her as she left her church to come to mine to witness my baptism. I pulled the card out and it was of a little sheep stranded on a stump of a tree in the middle of a pond of water. The caption read, "challenges".... And on the inside it read, ".....are the Shepherd's opportunities to prove His faithfulness again and again." Within the card was a check for $500.00 dollars, an anonymous person had provided me some funds to help me while I was unemployed. The verse on the card was from Psalms 57:3," He will send down help from Heaven...because of His love and His faithfulness."

I was overwhelmed by the generosity of this anonymous person how God must of moved upon their heart to be willing to bless me, and now that was a safety net to pay bills until I got my next job. I am so thankful for the body of Christ and how it works when you are in the center of His will. While I was driving off from church that day I heard this song by Chris Tomlin, "I will follow you"; this song really affirmed my desires. Go to YouTube and let it inspire you as well.

Thank you Lord, my Savior my Father and my God, step by step by step for ordering all my steps. Let me not worry about my future -- I give it and release it, for it is yours! I repent for trying to figure all out, what I must do next. I am waiting on your word for my next step. I will remain faithful in where I am at this time. Thank You for providing all my support, fill me with more faith and help me not doubt but rest in your promises to do good for me. I will keep my mind on thee and stay in perfect peace. Let Your love cover me and I will rest in the shadow of the Almighty, in his wings I will find my healing and comfort.

Chapter Fourteen

I AM

Life for me is fresh with new encounters and opportunities each day. I got the job at Newk's restaurant with Joseph's recommendations I passed all the other interviews with the other managers. I know The Lord has lead me here for a purpose and I am trusting he is indeed ordering my steps. It's good to be back into customer service I have worked in this area for over five years and the faces are all too familiar and the customers even recognize my voice not so my appearance at first because I am truly starting to transform, my hair is much longer and I am looking much healthier as well.

I do still struggle. When I am tired and rundown my flesh can fail me. I must be committed to surrendering my way all the time over and over. Life may not be consistent but I need to be. I need to keep taking my thoughts captive to the obedience of Christ. I must not dwell on the memories of the past. I have been struggling lately with my flesh and soul for I am craving to just being held. Close. A lot. When you have that for a long time it's a strange feeling not to experience it anymore. It is wonderful that The Lord knows my heart and my desires too. Psalms 37:4 tells us to take delight in The Lord, and He will give you the desires of your heart. I am learning so much by trusting and leaning in to Him.

This time when I was so feeling alone and wanting to be held close in the arms of a lover I fell asleep and I had this dream, and in the dream I was resting in someone's arms, I never saw the face but felt the security and peace in that embrace. As I was being held, I felt a hand stroking my hair and petting my head in such a loving way. When I woke up I felt so completed, rested and full and the craving I had before I went to bed was all gone, and I felt so satisfied in my soul. My dream had healed something in my soul. I really believe that the Holy Spirit felt my struggle and knew my desire and reached me in my dreams to fulfill an inner desire. I am so excited to trust in the power of the Spirit of God to touch me and minister to my needs and I can trust Him because I am finding He loves me and I am able to receive from Him more and more. I can trust Him to take care of my every need, small or great.

It seems every devotion I have read this year is constantly reminding me to totally trust the Father in all things. I've been so overwhelmed by His outpouring of real love and provisions. Today I went by my parent's house to see them, my mother was wanting me to have the money for my medications, and insulin isn't cheap.

Mother gave me fifty dollars to help me. I am in the process of getting set up on the program called "Needy Meds". When I went by the clinic that my church owned to get their address and information to enroll into the program, they let me know I didn't have to pay a hundred dollars to enter the program, that they had already entered me into it and I wouldn't have to pay anything but four dollars and sixty-nine cents for my monthly prescription for my insulin and other meds like blood pressure and iron. I was like WOW....GOD YOUR REALLY TAKING CARE OF ME! I was so overwhelmed at the grace I was given. Again The Lord provides all that I need.

Then the next night at small group the girls all gave me a card and collectively gave me a hundred and thirtyfive dollars, they all knew I had been in the hospital and had been out of work and they were so kind to provide me some funds to help me until I could start my new job, it would be two weeks before I got my first check. I was again feeling the love of the body of Christ and how wonderful it is to be loved by those who walk and live in the spirit of grace. God is supplying all my needs according to His riches, I am so blessed, in short I believe it is because I have committed my way to Yahweh, I am also committed to tithing and giving and being generous to others, either in deeds or when able with cash even if its two dollars to a man at the end of an exit ramp from the interstate or to my accountability partner or to bless my counselor with gift cards to her favorite restaurant because she has never charged me anything for her time, attention and kindness. I thank you Lord for reaching through your Body to touch and bless and affirm me through their obedience to give and pray for me. I love that you desire to love me.

It's been a couple of weeks now and I am really enjoying my new job. Everyone is pleasant and the managers seem grateful and actually work with us as a team. I even had the chance to pick up some extra hours because of a massive catering we got, funny thing it was for my church, the mega church I go to was having a conference we had to put together 4500 box lunches. I am off on the weekends so I could easily go and help out and hey its time and a half whether you worked forty hours or not so hey yeah I'm up for that. It was even fun thinking I was able to volunteer to help my own church and get paid at the same time too.

Today Is Sunday and its time to go to church and to blend in with the Body of Christ and sing our praise and release our sweet adoration to Him. The message was great, Pastor Chris teaching on grace from the book of Galatians. I am understanding now that faith is trust. I am on this journey to put all my trust in God the Father, God the son and God the Holy Spirit. The waiting is hard, the anticipation of breakthrough is frustrating at times and fights against my passions and desires.

Learning about how to die to my flesh and just wait on God to do what he has promised by surrendering …constantly it seems I am surrendering every time I turn around and laying down my way and to rest in His work not mine. I feel like it's raining and the sun is shining at the same time, I just know pass the clouds of doubt that there is hope and those beautiful blue skies. One scripture that stood out in today's sermon was Titus 2:11-12, Grace teaches us to say no to ungodliness and worldly passions and to live self-controlled, upright and godly lives.

Grace empowers me not to do what my flesh craves, I set my affections on Christ where my affections belong. Now, go to YouTube and look up David Crowder's "I am" and listen to how God is holding on to you as he has held me!

I am holding on to you in the middle of the storm I am holding on I am.

CHAPTER FIFTEEN

I am the Vine

It has been eleven months since I walked out of sin and walked into the Kingdom of God. It is spring, May and the first of the month when my rent is due and again I am still coming up short. I am broke, Still haven't gotten my first check from this new job of mine, one, they hold a pay period back and also take out for the uniforms given to you to get started. I felt I had to give in and call my Mother and just beg and ask her if she would write me a check for my rent and let me pay her back once my paycheck comes in, this is a hard thing for me to do, pride and fear of what my parents would think of me was a barrier to doing this. My Mother would often tell me when I said I needed to ask her something, she would cut me off and say, "as long as you're not asking for money ... because I aint got it for you". So, I called her up, feeling like I think God wants to reconnect and give my Mother at least an opportunity to be a part of helping me and being there for me for this season of my life. I was taken back that she actually agreed to help me…I mean I would get paid in two days but my rent was due today. So I ran across town to their house picked up the check then rushed to my apartment office to pay the rent, then rushed back to work to finish out my shift. Crazy day!! But I was blest to see God come through working in my parents to come to my assistance.

I was encouraged to reach out and contact my church through their financial assistance program that I might be able to benefit from. When I called the office they were quick to set me up with an appointment to meet with one of the financial counselors, I had to gather a lot of statements from my bank, so they could see my spending habits and bills. I had to get a copy of my rental agreement, I had to show my invoice statements of my car loan and just about every other expense along with a copy of my budget. They do this to weed out the serious from the hand outers they are very serious about helping people with debts and getting them debt free and financially responsible. When I met with my appointed counselor he was very impressed with my spending habits and how I really didn't live out of my means and how well I was doing despite coming up short, but most of that was because I had been in the hospital and sick missing work and I really was under employed in this economy. He could not even advise me to cut anything back…made me feel a lot better knowing I was really being responsible. As I left this meeting I really felt the peace of the Lord with me. I truly believe he is working all things out for my good, knowing I am entrusting all I am and all I am not into His Hands. I am willing to position myself to receive all that the Lord has for me, His presence, His provision, His passion, His desire to live through me as if I was a glove to His hand.

So much is going on it's like the month is getting away from me time flying. It's my birthday today, and so much has changed from last year's birthday. First of all I am a different person and I can see the changes myself as do those who knew me then and now.

I had the most delightful evening with some of my new and one of my oldest friends. It is so great to have key people in my life who pray and love and encourage me to keep on trusting in the Lord and this process of transformation to a new life in Christ.

My Counselor, yes the one I can't mention her name, the one who has to keep her anonymity, has been challenging me to consider about going through some inner healing thru a ministry she is involved in called "Restoring the Foundations". It's a process much like I experienced earlier in this year when I broke off soul ties that were made through sin. It is more in depth, going through a questionnaire and taking a look at one's ancestors and possible habitual sin habits and looking at areas in one's life where there is a lot of unforgiveness and possible ungodly beliefs along with possible demonic oppression. I really do want to work on issues that are barriers to me being able to connect to the Lord and my soul and spirit. She gave me the questionnaire to work on and told me to take my time and to pray over it and allow the Holy Spirit to speak and lead me in this process. She said she and her other intercessors would also be praying and fasting while I go through this process. It took me about a week to finish it, then my Counselor set up a time a night to meet at the church to go through the process and prayer. It really was a great experience to have some people there to pray over you and to be led by the Holy Spirit to release hurts and grudges of unforgiveness and to realize false beliefs that had bound me from really growing in truth. Thank you Lord for showing me areas and times from when I was young, how I was treated by my parents and others in my life and to be able to bring and see you there all along the way and to be able from my heart to forgive those who offended and hurt me and rejected me.

Thank you Lord for addressing the lies and revealing to me your truth, that I am your child and I am changing daily and I am like a rose blossoming in your presence. I have peace, love, joy and self-control. I feel like a new person captivated by your Grace in my life.

Okay, so each time God does a healing in my life whether in my soul or even my body it's like right away sin will crouch at the door! I find myself easily offended for or by others and I have to catch myself and see how my heart responds in all these situations for out of the heart the mouth speaks. I thank God I have great Christian friends that will listen and be so kind and compassionate about pointing out attitudes that they see and in love open my eyes to it, sometimes I can even see it as it is happening and repent quickly. One such time I remember after being promoted early at the restaurant I got to do the catering which was a huge responsibility and an opportunity to make tips sometimes big tips and sometimes no tips. Early in this position, I took a delivery to a repetitive client, and the company always tipped me and as I was bringing the order into this office it was two pretty big caterers for two different offices, well I passed the one who placed the order going out the door and she greeted me saying she had to run out but she left her credit card with the other lady who would signed for her order and I said okay, and I thanked her for the order. When the other lady signed for both orders and offered me payment she didn't even leave me a tip (which this big multimillion company always tipped) so I mention to her that Lisa always tipped us on the receipt. Well for over a 500.00 catering order she wrote down $ 5.oo and signed the receipt. I couldn't believe it! Instead of trusting The Lord for all things it just crawled all over and irritated me so much that when I got back to the car I just took my pen and turned that five dollar tip into a twenty five dollar tip, I just inserted a 2 in front of that 5. I felt like I was worth it! I was so offended of the jester of a 5dollar tip and I didn't think twice about it all day long.

I mean I didn't even hear or feel guilty, well not till after I got home and had some down time to rethink how my day went.

It wasn't until later that night when my Counselor called to see how I was doing and how my day was and it was like she could sense and even hear what was coming out of my heart about this whole ordeal that had happened, that she could address what was coming out of my heart; one that I was not trusting The Lord to be the provider of all my needs, and two the fear that I was missing something that was due me and three I actually was stealing by adding what was not given to me. Well, of course now I was feeling convicted and could see how fear and anger and a sense of entitlement was all coming out and even lying to my boss and if he found out about it I could face repercussions and possibly lose my position.

So, with my Counselor shining truth on my experience, and realizing how I had missed the mark, and knowing I had sinned, I began to pray and confess to the Father knowing as it says in the Bible, First John 1:9, If we (freely) admit that we have sinned and confess our sins, He is faithful and just (true to His own nature and promises) and will forgive our sins (dismiss our lawlessness) and (continuously) cleanse us from all unrighteousness (everything not in conformity to His will in purpose, thought, and action). Amplified version.

I felt a heaviness come off of me instantly. Then my Counselor pulled the carpet out from my feet and told me I should make restitution to this woman, it was after all her company credit card, and maybe they would notice sooner or later, and perhaps it would be a great way to be a witness to admit I had wronged them and how I had recently became a believer a Christian and how I failed to trust in The Lord and I wanted to repent from my actions and make it up to them and repay them the 25 dollars. Sounded easy, but was much harder to do. This company usually ordered from us every day. So I had it all planned out had the money in my pocket, but every day I kept missing Lisa, I even went one day on my off day to her office to see her but she was in a meeting and couldn't come down.

So, I just prayed and ask The Lord to open the door and help her be able to receive my apology when the time was right. It took like almost three weeks before I was able to see Lisa again. When I did get the opportunity it was again a huge order and for like three different offices at this company and so I asked Lisa if I could get her to step away here for just two minutes so I could tell her something. Well like I said it was like three weeks ago so I had to remind her how she had passed me in the parking lot that one day when she said another person had her credit card to pay for her order, and I had told her how the lady only gave me a 5 dollar tip and how it had offended me and I without thinking about it just changed it to 25 dollar tip and how later on I became so convicted about that action and told her I had recently became a born again Christian and I realized that I not only reacted wrong and I had not trusted The Lord to provide for me in all things but I stepped in and did what I thought in my own eyes was owed to me in and through what was really taking and stealing that which was not freely given to me.

Well, then I braced myself for her response knowing it could turn out all wrong with some severe consequences. Lisa just looked at me and then said she appreciated the honesty and conviction and said she had really not had the time to look over the invoices and did not realize that the other woman only gave me a 5 dollar tip. She said we usually only give 5 dollar tips because we order pretty much every day from your restaurant, but she remember it was an unusual larger order than what they normally do, and that even though I was giving her the cash back she didn't have a way to attach it back to the company credit card and she insisted I keep it and not think any more about it and we would carry on from this moment on and she forgave me and it was a learning experience for both of us. Now that is some Grace!! I was so relieved and I learned a lot from that experience. Trusting and not over-reacting to others actions.

I was reminded about the story Jesus was telling his disciples, when He was revealing to them I AM the Vine. Catch for us the foxes, the little foxes that ruin the vineyards, our vineyards that are in bloom. (Song of Solomon 2:15)

A Christian is a branch in The Vine, (John 15: 1-6) Jesus is the vine and we are the Branches who is joined to Christ, united to Him and deriving life from Him, and He is a participant of His very own nature. (2Peter 1:4) It is the Lord that causes me to bear forth much fruit and it comes by His doing, not mine. (Hosea 14:8) The Holy Spirit is the manifestation of this fruit, it flows from the branches through its branches.

The foxes are the sins of our flesh. (2Corinthians 7:1) The foxes are gross sins like murder, drunkenness, adultery, fornication, idolatry, see Galatians 5:19, for the whole list.

The little foxes are the sins of our flesh that creep into us little by little unchecked or unnoticed and spoil the vine and take our fruit away. There are three kinds of sins of the spirit/soul; the wrong things we think, the wrong things we say and the wrong things we do. Heart sins, lip sins and behavior sins. The heart sins may be secret sins, like jealousy, pride, impurity. These sins hinder the fruit in our lives.

God see our secret sins, Psalms 90:8, in His presence they are brought to light. The lip sins are an unruly and an undisciplined tongue and it does some great damage, for example: lying, being critical, or tattle- tale- baring. Then there are behavior sins, where we act out and it's obvious even to others. We have an unclean heart and a wrong spirit when we are unkind, thoughtless or harsh toward others or when we are in a wrong relationship with another person. These little foxes and all foxes for that manner must be rounded up and put to death.

(Gal.5:24) And realize this, little foxes will grow to be big foxes before long.

So, how do we kill them you ask? Read Judges 15:4-5. We set them to fire! No, really, spiritually we bind them all up and ask the Holy Spirit to set His fire upon them, we repent we surrender and ask for them to all be under the atonement of the blood of Jesus.

We all have little foxes in our life that steal the life out of us and stifle the flow of life producing fruit. We deal with this by confession of our sins knowing and trusting that Jesus will cleanse us from all unrighteousness. (1john1:9)

We have to consistently take captive of all thoughts to the obedience to Christ and renewing our mind to allow the Holy Spirit reveal to us not condemn but convict us of all sins so we can come to the throne of Grace by confession in Jesus name and allow the Holy Spirit to fill us up with His presence and restore us back to abundant life and before long we will see our lives blooming again and producing fruit.

I am so glad when we come to Christ we don't have to have our lives all together. He takes all our brokenness and strife when we surrender to Him and give Him Lordship over our lives. He begins to make something beautiful of our life. All my confusion I surrender and He brings me understanding and a peace the world can never know.

When He sets us apart for the sanctification process He does not isolate us, He brings in the right person or persons at the right time to help us and guide us with truth and grace. The flip side is the enemy will try to cause us to separate or distract us by work, or sickness or isolation to miss out from church through all kinds of circumstances. Mine would be sickness and injuries that would pop up from out of the blue. The way to stay in peace through being set apart is to constantly watch out for what your focus is and to guard against what you look at and listen to, like for me I had to cut out TV and magazines. Once you open your eyes to that stuff it is easy to open a door for evil spirits to harass you and lead you into temptations and ultimately to actually sinning. That is why we have to be diligent to guard our hearts for out of it flows the issues of life. (Proverbs 4:23) There is an old song from the 1980's that John Michael Tolbert sang, look it up on YouTube "I am the Vine".

I am the Vine and you are the Branches, lean in me and you will never die

I am the Vine and my Father is the keeper, come to me, let the Spirit bring you Life.

CHAPTER SIXTEEN

Good Good Father

It is July 4th and most of my friends are gone to the beach or on some kind of three day weekend. I am off work and no plans. I was also realizing it would have been my anniversary of 16 years to my EX. I had to rethink that thought and tell myself it's been over a year now and I can celebrate my liberation out of darkness into God's marvelous light. I didn't know how this day would soon come to test that very truth.

I was glad to get a call from my Counselor, she had gotten off work early and was wondering if I wanted to meet her at her parent's house once again to eat and celebrate the Fourth. I was like sure I don't have any plans I am in!

While I was driving my vehicle my check engine light came on and as I was going up this incline a small mountain, my car started to smoke and it just quit on me and I couldn't get it started. So, I called my Friend The Counselor on her cell phone and asked her if she didn't mind to come and get me my car broke down.

Well we went on to her parent's house to eat and after visiting her family for a while I asked her to run me to Walmart I think my car needs oil. So we went in got the oil then went to the car tried to get it started again and it would not crank. I remembered I had an extended warranty I bought and I grabbed the papers out of the glovebox and praying that it was still valid. Well thank God it was! So it was late and the car rental place was closed so I called my friend Beth to see if she could let me use her work truck until I could get a rental car and she was so generous to say yes sure, come and get it. So I called a wrecker to come and take my car to the dealer, which cost a hundred dollars, but then I realized I had insurance that would cover towing so I would get reimbursed for that.

Knowing I knew The Lord was testing my heart with this clear interruption and inconvenience I quickly asked Him to settle my mind and heart, again another opportunity to trust Him with all that I had. I remember telling him that I had surrendered my life to Him and that all that I had was His and as He was my Father I asked Him to help me in this situation. He certainly was, by providing great friends like Beth and my Counselor. I finally was able to get a rental car for a few days. When the dealership called from where I bought the vehicle, the service advisor told me they would have to tear the engine down and I had to give authority to break down the engine to find the problem, if it was a warranty issue then the extended warranty would cover all charges but if it was not a covered item I would have to pay the three hundred dollars out of my pocket and pay for the rental car as well.

So I consented, it had to be done to find the problem, as it turned out it was my engine and it looked like abuse, from the warranty Inspector's perspective, which meant I was liable to pay for all repairs that amounted up to five thousand dollars and then would include extra charge for the rental bill. I was so disturbed in this news I told him I would have to call him back. I found myself overwhelmed and depressed and tired of being so needy, I then immediately turned off all distractions and got before The Lord and laid all my burdens and concerns before

Him. I didn't have five thousand dollars, much less the three hundred just from the initial diagnostics. I had just bought this car over a year ago, I had done the maintenance, and I had receipts of oil changes how could the vehicle be in this condition?

I thanked The Lord for being my provider in all that I had gone through. The enemy was screaming in my head "now what you gonna do?" "You can't even take care of yourself!" "How are you going to make it?"

I at first was responding with fear, confusion and a whole lot of "I don't knows". Then I realized it. I was leaning on my own reasoning….not faith. I told the lies in my head and all the questions, I know what I am going to do, I am going to trust my Father, he is my protector and my provider, He has not disappointed me once since I began this journey and I guess He will do what He has always done in the past. He has constantly provided all my needs according to His riches in Christ Jesus! He is for me and not against me and He holds no good thing for those who love Him. When trials come or tests we must not turn to human reasoning to answer the doubts or accusations or temptations to fix or control our lives. No, we must follow our Shepherd and Lover of our souls, we do as he did, and we come against the taunts and temptations like firey darts thrown at us from the enemy by speaking and declaring the written word of God. So I worshiped The Lord for a while, and then while I was praying for His favor I heard in my spirit, speak and declare what you want, so I did. I didn't want to owe anything only what is due according to my extended warranty, my deductible. I literally asked The Lord, "what do you want me to do about this, how should I handle it"? Then, He said, "Go to the used car manager that sold me the car and the warranty and tell him what has transpired." So I went to the service department to check and see the service advisor and he showed me my engine and how it was overfilled with oil, I interrupted him and said, "well that I did do, I thought I was low so I added to it but I forgot I was on a uphill mountain, but I never drove it, I had it towed from where I was because it still didn't start". The advisor even suggested it could have been done by the previous owner. It didn't matter the warranty inspector said it was not warrantable. I said I will be right back. I then went and did as The Lord had told me. I marched right over to the use car manager and asked to speak to him. He remembered me and ask how he could help me. I told Him of all the events that led up to now and he said I know that inspector, let me go look at your vehicle and talk to the service advisor and I will personally call the inspector. He said why don't you go home and I will call you in an hour. I thought to myself, yeah, an hour right... but I didn't want to sit around that dealership either so I said ok I will be waiting for your call.

Exactly an hour later the used car manager called me and said, "Ms. Broom, I got it covered for you". He told me, all I would have to pay was the one hundred dollar deductible, which with the reimbursement from the towing I would have. I said what about the rental charges? He said,"covered."

I was so blown away that it all was taken care of. I started thanking The Lord for doing it again, always coming through, what a Good Good Father I have!! God, my God is so faithful to me! I am blessed, a billion thank- yous for His mercy and great grace unto me. YouTube Chris Tomlin, "Good, Good Father".

Oh I have heard a thousand stories of what of what they think you're like, but I've heard the tender whisper of love in the dead of night

CHAPTER SEVENTEEN

Through it all

It is amazing how far I have come in my journey with my decision to follow Jesus. At this present writing it's been almost three years since I answered the call to follow the Lord, tho no one go with me.

Through it all it has been step by step, falling and getting up again, purposing in my heart to live a life of surrender to a loving God, who loved me more than I could ever comprehend. Coming away from the world and shutting off all the distractions and fasting from the pleasures of this world to gain the contentment and fulfillment of His kingdom. This is the sanctification process. I have experienced His presence.

The word says you must come to Him by faith, that is what pleases our Father. The word also says in Revelation 3:20 That The Lord stands at the door and knocks and if you hear his voice and (key word hear) opens the door and invites me in I will come in and eat with that person and he with me.

Through it all, from being a disappointment to my parents going through such rejection and now seeing how the enemy planted so many seeds in my upbringing and how the enemy was also out to steel my identity and how I bought into the lies one after another how he was out to destroy and ultimately kill me, how much more grateful for the Light of God who came to Redeem me and take me for His very own! He does leave the ninety-nine to come after the one who is gone from His fold. He knows that we are His and He does not forget or forsake any follower that is His.

I knew of The Lord from when I was a child, I had just grown up being offended and wounded by the ones that were close to me. I was looking for love in all the wrong faces and ultimately leaving and going after the world's love and acceptance, thinking I knew what I was doing and it was the best for me. I was definitely a prodigal, going after all the gusto I could get for myself. I lived a self-center life full of pride and arrogance with a terrible attitude full of anger and rage if I didn't get what I wanted for me or at times for the ones I loved.

I look back and through it all I can see The Lord's wooing me and drawing me away to look for Him, from the disappointments, the death of my brother, to having my whole world turn upside down, from coming into the saving knowledge of who Jesus Christ is, to answering His invitation, to allowing Him to come into my open door of my heart and watching Him time after time heal the wounds and memories of my past to give me a future and a Hope in Him…..called Life. I did all I could do to undo me and He still pursued me followed me to catch me and to turn me around to follow him, going the distance to save me from myself. He found me and picked me up and kept me close to His heart and brought me back to the fold of the beloved.

You know I have heard there is an equation to worship; The size of your praise is directly proportional to the magnitude of the hell God took you out of! (Samuel Rodriguez)

Following the Lord is a step by step adventure choosing to believe in Him and then entrusting your life into His hands.

Will you ask yourself, am I totally surrendered to God and do I believe in Jesus? Do I have an intimate relationship or do I have an empty dusty religion?

If you will ask the Holy Spirit to come and open the door that no man can shut and if you will ask Jesus to reveal Himself to you, then He will. It starts with the first step, then all you have to do is confess you are a sinner and then ask the Lord Jesus to come into your heart He will forgive you and wash you from all your sins however many or deep or serious He wipes your slate clean and will give you the garment of salvation and a robe of righteousness (Isaiah 61:10). Then your journey will begin, step after next step. You will not regret it. Know this too, Jesus will never disappoint you. You may disappoint yourself, others may let you down or even abandon you but Jesus never fails you or leaves you.

You owe yourself to ask for the Truth, search for it and you will find it and when you find it, the Truth will set you free. We can and must not put our confidence in any flesh for mere man will disappoint us at times.

In my journey into the heart of Jesus, He lead me to see the Father, that's why Jesus came to bring us all back into a relationship and back to where we were all supposed to be part of the kingdom and the family of God.

Father God is more than the Creator of the universe, more than just Holiness, He wants to have a relationship with each of us and be the Father of all fathers. He is our protector, provider, and the one who affirms us. I have struggled to come to know who I am in Christ, but he has led me through life's experiences and taught me at every place just how He wants me to see who He is in any situation. Homosexuality was just the tip of the iceberg for me, I had a lot more issues underneath hidden. Just like a caterpillar grows through stages to be a beautiful butterfly, at times its slow, it's dark and it seems lonely but God is continually growing me, and all of us.

We can't interrupt the process each stage of the growth process is vital for our future. Sometimes the process is painful but it always has its purpose, we must in these times lean in hard and not ignore the lesson.

Our life lessons leads us to become overcomers and more than conquers through the power of the Holy Spirit. We can casually walk on the edge of the beach or we can choose to go deeper into the ocean of God's love and purpose by going ankle to knee to waist to fully submerged into the ocean being carried away by its current. The greatest thing I came to know is that He was there through it all. My mission goal is 1Peter 1:15&16,

BUT AS HE WHO CALLED YOU IS HOLY,

YOU ALSO BE HOLY IN ALL YOUR CONDUCT, SINCE IT IS WRITTEN,

"YOU SHALL BE HOLY, FOR I AM HOLY".

My holiness is God's supreme purpose for my life. More than a responsibility an astounding privilege that The Holy One should choose me earthbound, frail, and flawed as I am, that He should cleanse me

from all my sins fill me with His Holy Spirit, and then use me to reflect the splendor of His Holiness in this dark, dark world.

CHAPTER EIGHTEEN

I Am Redeemed

It's time to renew my rental agreement for my studio apartment this month. Of course each year it will continue to go up fifteen dollars. If you don't renew in a certain time period it even goes up more like fifty dollars and then even a hundred dollars after the renewal date. I have been praying about it and I have had to trust The Lord anyway for my rent every month so what's wrong with trusting Him to provide another fifteen dollars? So, I just went and re-signed for another year, knowing He holds my future.

This summer I had the privilege to meet and get to hear my Counselor's mentor Jane Anderson, she came to one of our bible studies to speak. I took in every word she spoke. The most I got from that night was how we cannot depend on our human reasoning, but we can depend on the truth of God. Human reasoning is what put us in a disadvantage from the garden, Eve looked at the fruit and thought in her mind it was good to eat.

God had already spoken to Adam and Eve and told them the truth, but when the opportunity presented itself they both chose to believe a lie. Sin has devastating effects when we sin against God. Like death, separation, confusion, loneliness and isolation. I can hear Jane say, "don't get mad at the only one who can change your heart."

After that bible study and talking to my Counselor, she told me my next step was working on my Testimony, my conversion experience when I surrendered my life to Jesus. She said Jane was really good at helping people put together their testimonies down to a short concise layout so you could share it with people who you meet in and out of your day to laying it out in a format to share to an audience. So I was like okay sounds good, and so we met on a Saturday and we discussed a lot about my background and how I came to know that I was saved. Then Jane shared with me an outline she used to write it all down. You know, like my life before Christ, what events led me to Christ and how my life had changed after giving my life to Christ. So, I was to spend some time writing it all out and then she would meet me again to go over and critique it once I finished it and so we both worked on it, once I gave it to her, we polished it off over lunch a couple of Saturdays later. I really enjoyed that day and she encouraged me and told me she really liked my testimony and only had one verse she wanted me to inject into it and that was John 1:12;"but as many received him, to them gave he the right to become the children of God, even to them that believe on his name." (American Standard Version).

We talked along time sharing from each other's life, I could tell she really cared. I told her I really appreciated my Counselor, her friend and all of her counsel, that I looked to her as a spiritual Mother, and now getting to know you, I feel like I am talking to my spiritual Grandmother! She laugh at that one.

I didn't realize that this would be the last time I would see and talk to Jane Anderson. Just a week after this meeting she had some back pain and finally went to see about it and found out She had been walking around with stage 4 lung cancer. I believe it was like five weeks later she passed on into Eternity, and she did it with such amazing grace. She had just told me a few weeks ago that it is The Lord who orders all our steps and He knows all our days. I was sad that I didn't get to know her better but she was known by a lot of people and I hear of some of the things she has taught from others. So it really was like she was a grandmother of the Faith to me. Before she passed away she had encouraged me to get involved in a community bible study that she was a leader and founder. It was a nine month study, this year it was on Daniel and Revelation. She told me she would make sure I got a great group leader, she taught the day classes and her friend Kelly taught the night classes. Jane passed away as the first classes started, people were very sad. When I came in to register for the CBS (Community Bible Study), I was told my registration had already been paid up ….by Jane. She really wanted me to get involved in this group of ladies of all ages and backgrounds. It was a great experience and I will always be grateful for the short time I got to spend with her, she really made an impression on my life.

After some weeks going to this study on the book of Daniel I was awoken in my sleep and I heard the Spirit say to me, "Write this down", so I got up and got my journal and wrote this.

"It is by no coincidence that you are in a study about Daniel. It is the Lord's purpose. You are a child of God in whom there is no blemish, you are well favored, skillful in all wisdom. You are called to be like Daniel— to purpose in your own heart not to defile yourself while in this "captivity". Being in a place like "Babylon" I can still have favor and kindness from the hand of The Lord. I must try to not indulge in the excess, I must try to keep my body, soul and mind pure without defilements. God is the one in complete control over Times, Seasons, and positions and my destiny".

As the end of the year 2015 was coming to an end and a New Year was arriving once again I heard the Holy Spirit say to me that this year would be a year of new connections. I thought okay, so are you telling me to get more involved with the singles in my church and get into a small group with singles? I decided to join a couple of small groups one monthly and one weekly where singles would meet up. I was so surprised when I went to a few of the meetings, there were a lot of people my own age and not as nearly as many twenty somethings as I would of thought. I met some wonderful people with great testimonies, I thought this was what the Lord was leading me to do until I got a call from my Aunt.

It was about three months after when I was talking to my Aunt that she told me my Uncle had been saying for months that I should move to Oklahoma and live with them. She told her husband wait, we need to pray about that, whether it is of the Lord's will or not. I didn't need to up root myself from my church my new friends or apartment and my counselor. So we decide to pray about it, I mean I had already signed a year's lease on my studio apartment and it would have to be God for me to get out of it and still get my hefty deposit back.

Then there is the question what about my medical situation I was on a year program where I got my insulin for barely nothing. Then also me telling my Mom and Dad about me moving away out of state.

Well I had to talk to my counselor right away on this opportunity and she thought it was a very good thing for me to think about and consider. So we all began to pray that if this is the direction that The Lord was leading me that he would open all the doors for me to walk thru.

That Saturday I ended up going to the apartment office to speak with the general manager about getting out of my lease.

He looked up my file and said there was a part of the agreement he couldn't find that would cause me to pay an early release fee but he couldn't find it in my contract. So, he told me as long as I gave him sixty days I would get my whole deposit back and I would not have to pay any extra fees because it wasn't in my contract. Wow! Well there's the first open door sign right there. That doesn't happen much, and besides I would need the sixty days just to get my move organized. The next test would be on securing me some insulin until I got a new job and some health insurance.

I went to the Dream Center to see if it would be possible for them to transfer my special program for prescriptions and after some calling we found out it was not transferable. I would have to register in Oklahoma to see if I could qualify. That week at our "First Wednesday" service at church the guest speaker for the church service was Craig Groeschel, from Oklahoma, sounded like another confirmation to me.

Later on that weekend I was over Beth and Drenda's house and I felt the Lord prod me to ask Drenda if she had a little extra insulin pens to hold me over if I was to move to my Aunts place until I could get out there and find a doctor and a job, and without flinching she was all over it to my surprise she came up from basement where she kept her insulin in a separate refrigerator with about six months supply of insulin for me to have I was so blown away at her generosity. Well as it worked out the doors and the pathway seem clear to me that this is where my journey was going.

I turned in a six week notice at work so they could fill my position and I started packing and purging once again. I didn't have much, but I could only take what my SUV could hold. I was able to sell my futon bed at the last minute that was a blessing. Jane had given me a little red antique desk that I wanted to keep and that was able to fit with just a few wall pictures and lots and lots of books and my TV. I gave away a lot and donated some things as well. The Lord worked it all out the big and little details.

As I look back and recount all the blessings and provisions that the Lord has all worked out it is so overwhelming how much He loves me. From the moment He called me to just take Him at His word and to just believe it, even if I had reservations or different beliefs, He challenged me to read the Word and believe it and as I did I came to see Jesus come alive and see how it was all about Him.

Then the next year He told me to just trust Him and at first I was so all about that idea of trusting Jesus, then I realized I was probably going to be in a lot of tight situations where I was going to really have to depend on The Lord, and as it was I did go through a series of events that it looked like every month I would be so needy, but God showed up every time as my good good Father who never let me down and never ran out on me.

Little did I realize The Lord would be leading and opening and closing doors for me to move to Oklahoma to live with family. I am in the season of making new connections. Moving to Oklahoma has totally made me be in circumstances to make new connections. I was led to get a job where my Uncle works, the number one security business in the world. Only God could order these steps for me to get a perfect schedule working Monday thru Friday from seven to three. I get to work in a beautiful high rise building and greet people and encourage people all the time. I have time to pray and listen and be taught daily; it truly is the perfect job for me and God knew it and led me there and has given me such favor with the people I get to work for and with.

I have had several "encounters" with the God Head, the Father, the Son and the Holy Spirit. He is for real and He is supernatural and able to connect to us. It was not too long ago while I was at work on a football Saturday that I had a tremendous encounter with the Holy Spirit. I was working an extra job doing security for one of the college football teams here in Oklahoma. While I was riding in the company van enjoying the early morning sunrise and in my heart just praising and thanking the Lord for such a glorious experience in seeing this, I took a picture with my cell phone and immediately shared it with some close friends. The radio was playing country classic songs, and as I was listening I heard the Holy Spirit say to me to listen to what I was hearing and start picking out the lies in these songs. "Looking for Love in all the wrong places" was one of the songs, and of course I knew I wasn't looking in wrong places anymore, but I knew LOVE was looking for me. When we got to the college and got our assignments for our post to be guarding I usually got the same post every Saturday, where I was with about four other guards and we got to watch the TV and watch the game and we had Wi-Fi and plenty of food from the tailgaters. Well this particular Saturday, I got a different post where I was the only guard in this architecture building and I had no TV, I had no internet and no Wi-Fi. So here I am all by myself and 12 hours on my hand to guard the doors to a building that no one was even trying to come through. I had been putting on the back burner a lot of memories from like 30 and 40 years ago, so realizing I had all this time on my hands and I was all by myself I decided to take advantage of this opportunity and pray and worship the Lord and just sit down and ask Him questions. I began by asking Him why was He bringing up all these memories here lately from like 40 years ago? And then I heard Him say, "Terrie, I AM bringing all these things up as you can handle them so that you can forgive those who have took advantage of you, those who have hurt you, those who have disappointed you to those who have abandoned you, so that when I get through healing your soul you will not have anything in common with those who sinned and caused you to be wounded in your soul. You will not be pulled back into lust or fear or the spirit of Homosexuality, or pride. I will be able to use you and you will not be pulled back into those areas anymore because I AM healing your soul. So with each memory, we had all day, I asked the Lord to forgive each person He brought to my heart and I asked the Lord to forgive me for holding these things against those people for such a long time. Then out of the blue my mom called me and the Lord must of healed something in me because we had the longest conversation ever, it lasted about 2o minutes and at the end of the call my mom told me she loved me and for the first time I said I loved her too and I actually meant it and felt it for the first time....now that was a miracle!

Then Sunday night as I was lying in bed I was not quite asleep still alert and just pondering all that had happened during the weekend, I felt a breeze come into my bedroom. The door was closed and the fan was off. I had my eyes closed just resting. Then the breeze turned up and I felt a gust of wind blowing in my room until it turned into like tornadic winds, I was afraid to open my eyes, I tried to get up and I could not move at all, not my shoulders or my head. I was trying to get up and out of the bed but I was penned down with this force of wind. I started yelling for help hoping my Aunt and Uncle would hear, but no, no one heard me. I was yelling like you do through a box fan and all I could hear is myself, then it dawned on me that this must be the Holy Spirit! So then my yell for help changed to yelling for more and more and bring it on all the more!! I felt so rested and peaceful it was a true encounter and the power of God falling on me. I will never forget it. He desires us to be free and healed in our spirit, soul and body. I came to Him in my desperation of needing to know Truth. I started seeking Him looking and listening and I had a desire to be and do something to make a difference in the Kingdom of

God. Jerimiah 29:13 says, "And you will seek me and find me, when you search for me with all your heart."

I pray that as you have read my story it encourages you to know that it's never too late to surrender your life to a Holy God who is and has always been your Father, just come home to Him while you can. Just like a prodigal I left out to a foreign land to indulge in pleasure and looking for love in all the wrong places, coming to my senses to realize I left my true identity as a child of God where I was always loved and had pleasures available all the while, to live a life of selfishness all for my own.

Turn away from the lies the enemy tells you, to keep you from experiencing the freedom and love of God. He sent his one and only begotten Son to lay His life down as a sacrifice for all mankind, that's you and me. It's by confession of Him as Lord, and believing in your heart that you are born again. You must decide to follow Jesus, no turning back, tho no one goes with you, the cross before you and the world behind you... no turning back. If you surrender everything you are and everything you are not and ask Jesus into your heart and ask the Holy Spirit to come live in you, you will be led by Him and if you believe right you will live right.

Find a solid foundational spirit filled church and dig in get involved and if needed get a mentor or counselor to help disciple you into The Truth of God's word who will invest time and pray with you to follow after The Lord with all your being.

It is my personal belief that if you have an encounter with the living God your life will transform and you will live a godly life in peace and great love. This is my song, this is my story. Check out this last important song on YouTube, it is my testimony as well as others. Look for "I am Redeemed" on YouTube, by Big Daddy Weave.

Chapter Nineteen

Come to the table

It's March 25th,2017 it early Saturday morning and my phone rings waking me from my sleep. It is my Mother, "Terrie, this is Mom, are you up?" I was thinking, I am now…but I said "yes", "what's up? She said "I am calling to let you know your Brother passed away sometime in the middle of night. I was stunned, not really shocked. I mean we all knew he was not well, the year before he has a 5 by-pass open heart surgery and he struggled with pain and it was hard on him. I think we all knew one day we were going to wake up and find him just as he died, in his sleep. We didn't know if he had a heart attack or another stroke, we just knew his life was over. I tried to comfort my Mom on the phone and told her I would leave as soon as I could to get home and be there for the Funeral which turned into a Memorial because my parents wanted Ronald cremated.

After the Memorial I headed back to Oklahoma back to my routine, it was like two weeks in and I clearly heard the Holy Spirit speak to me.

I will never forget it, this conversation through my intellect said "get ready to purge through your things again and start packing, I need you to move back home, your Dad is not going to live much longer."

I was like "really"? I just got here a year ago I just got all settled in and life is good. I started thinking I can't go home and live with my parents. Ugh, is this You God?

Surely this is the devil trying to mess with my mind, surely The Lord wouldn't want this for me! Then I said if this is You Lord please give me a sign, some scripture to hold on to. Then it's like the Holy Spirit just started to comfort me and say to my spirit, I didn't say you had to move in with your parents. Here is a word for you look up John 14. So I did, I started at verse one.

As I read those two verses I felt such peace and comfort, and confirmation that this indeed was The Lord's will for me. It took me like a month to start purging stuff, not that I had a lot but once again doing away with unnecessary stuff and organizing for the move back and also having to tell my Aunt and Uncle about my new plans was not going to be easy for they liked having me there especially my Uncle because I was there for him a lot while he was working at night to stay around close for my Aunt.

I was blessed enough to be able to transfer with my job, Birmingham has a home office of my security company I was able to move home and start the next day, just had to stop by and get uniforms and sign some papers and I was good to go. What I didn't count on was before I left it probably was like six weeks from when The Lord had told me to move back to Alabama and I had called and asked if I could move home til I could find a place and Mom was like you can stay here if you want and use your brother's old room. So I was okay with that, so I thought.

I had not visited my parent's house for a long time, I had no idea the conditions they were living in. When I had arrived home with my car packed with all that I owned I found my

Parents had turned into hoarders, to my astonishment they had holes in the ceiling and plumbing issues to where you couldn't take a shower or bath, clutter all over the place they didn't even turn on the lights I presume so they didn't have to look at the dust. The couch was the only safe place and at night you could hear rats running a muck in the ceilings and walls. Roaches everywhere my skin was literally crawling I was like how could this be the will of God for me to live here! I tried to get my mom to clear our one room for me but both my parents would not let me get rid of anything of great significance to make it livable for me. I started complaining about this, I was getting pretty upset, I prayed and ask the Holy Spirit what and where and how? I just could not stay here and you brought me back to this? What is up are you training me for a third world mission trip or what?

You need to tell me what to do or where to go because I can't do this like THIS. Then, when I calmed down and settled my heart I heard The Holy Spirit say to my spirit,"I didn't say you were to move into your parent's house I said I would prepare a place for you. Call Chris. I thought Chris? Okay, Chris was a small group leader I had a couple of years ago, I often dog sat and house sat for her when she travelled. So I went with the prompting and I called Chris and just said hey I am back in Birmingham now and I am in a rock and a hard place and told her of what had all transpired and I asked her if by chance if she would be up to renting me a place in her space and having a roommate? She responded by letting me know she had just started recently praying about getting a roommate. In which I let her know I was indeed the answer to that prayer, for the Holy Spirit had told me to call her and ask her about just that!! How great is that! God is a good, good Father once again.

It was while I was living with Chris The Holy Spirit would do another great work of healing in my life.

One evening I had come home and I was so hungry. I came in from working and I was in such a hurry to make my dinner and as I was scarfing it down so fast a thought came to my mind and I heard, "Your eating like an Orphan". I was like what?

Then again I heard, "YOU are eating like an Orphan".

I thought I had gone through all the inner healing one could go through and now I see there is still a piece of me in my soul that still needed to be healed, my Orphan Mind set. This is not a demon that I needed to be cast out, but a false belief system that I had attached my own identity to and now it has become a spiritual stronghold in my life.

So I began really looking into what an Orphan mind set was really about. What it is: A Lie, one that I believed was a truth, I could see it all in me. I was living in such a place and struggled all my life like I was an Orphan. I felt I was alone even in a crowed room, like I was looking from the outside in. I never felt like I belonged in my family. I wasn't close to my brothers I wasn't close to my Parents. I didn't have a home I could call home anymore. I felt pretty much alone and on my own.

I often felt like I had to take care of myself, self- sufficiency, if I was going to have anything I had to go out and get it. My Parents on the outside looked like great parents but they were hurting themselves, My Mother has been abandoned by her own Father at birth, and my Father had Meningitis as a 6 year old and was in isolation for almost 2 years, it greatly affected their lives and in turn wounded their children's lives. They were detached from us. They often said love was a roof over your head, a meal in your mouth and bed to sleep in. I never liked that definition. Sure they met my outward needs but never met my emotional needs of affirmation. I grew up thinking I was one of the boys. I was tough and had a streak of rebellion in me. When I was in the seventh grade I didn't want to go on a field trip so I told the teacher I couldn't go on the trip because I couldn't afford it for my family was in a financial bind. I spoke and declared that on my life; a curse of poverty and I didn't even realize it. There in my early childhood the Enemy would plant seeds of deception, one being I was one of the boys, and I was poor, and I wasn't loved. There the strongholds were planted in my mind. I didn't feel valued or loved and that's where fear entered my life. I tried earnestly to be outgoing and be a good friend to my peers I craved attention. This kind of thinking opened the door for the enemy to come through and build a very strong place in my mind by constantly believing and exchanging the Truth for a lie a deception of who I really was and Am.

This is how the enemy works, He plants seeds in our minds. Seeds of doubt, rejection, abandonment, of poverty, seeds of delusion, seeds of lust of wrong identity, seeds of hate and anger. The earlier it takes root the stronger the stronghold. The Enemy is counting on us to keep a hard heart and be unforgiving and not willing to listen to the good news of The Gospel of God. God is so merciful and gracious to us, He woos us by the power and presence of His Spirit. He will speak through people we come in contact with, He uses situations and circumstances in our lives to get our attention to prick our hearts to call out to Him.

Living with an Orphan mind set or mentality makes you very immature in the way that you live. For me I can look back and see how selfish and self- centered I was. I see how dependent and co-dependent I was to many people that came in and out of my life. I struggled with the fear of rejection and became a performer to gain acceptance from the people I was attracted to and wanted their approval from as well.

During this time I slipped back to gambling, in my mind I thought since I was a Christian I could just take The Holy

Spirit with me and cross the boundaries and go after the enemy's territory to gain back some lost dividends and praying for God's protection as I went. When driving back home I really sensed The Holy Spirit convicting me over what I had done. He said He protected me this time, but I wasn't to use or call on Him to use Authority in that way. He reminded me of the scripture where Simon saw the Apostles doing miracles, and he wanted to buy that power from them. Apparently living in this mindset condition I found myself falling back into a behavior I had once lived in. While talking to my counselor she called me out on it and as I was not aware, some other people in my circle of influence had noticed me as well. My counselor asked me if I wanted to go through another SOZO encounter. I said yes. I didn't want to live in self-sufficiency and trying to meet my needs. I started to realize I wasn't trusting and relying on The Lord to provide for me in His way and His timing. So after a few weeks we set up a time and I met my counselor with some other people to walk through a SOZO session. I was able to repent of my behavior and denounce lies that I thought were true, I was able to forgive certain people that I believed in who had wounded my soul.

I felt such a release and beak through, I felt so refreshed. It wasn't long after this that my roommate asked me to move out, she had plans on putting her house on the market so like within two weeks I had to move out and find another place. I knew this was just another test on trusting The Lord. I positioned myself to surrender and lean in to trust In His provision and plan. I even went to my Pastor and his wife to ask them to pray for me and pray a blessing over me. Life for me was looking kinda dismal. Even before my roommate had asked me to move out I was groaning in my spirit to have a place of my very own. I looked and looked for studio apartments for rent, but most of them stayed filled because of college students and the one I did find was in a sketchy area and the more I thought about it, the studio apartment was so small I felt like it was like a jail cell. For about a week I camped out in my SUV in the back of a nice Church parking lot, until a cop came driving through.

My friend Wendy called me checking in on me and I told her I was living in my car she didn't like that idea and she offered me to come and stay with her for a couple of months, enabling me to save money to move into an apartment soon. While I was saving money and praying about a place of my own I felt like The Holy Spirit was leading me to buy a condo or townhouse. I felt the prompting to call a mortgager and see if I could get preapproved and I did qualify.

It just made better sense to buy and not rent, because the rent always goes up at renewal time. I felt this was the Lord letting me know he is listening to my prayers.

By the first of May I had to find another landing place for Wendy was going as a missionary to Africa and she needed the time and space to get ready for that. I wasn't going to freak out or get anxious or mad, by now I realized I had a choice in all things I could choose to leave it in my Father God's hands or try to do everything in my own so called wisdom. I just did what I knew to do until The Lord intervene on my behalf. He remind me He was going before me to prepare a place for me and He reminded me that He has many dwelling places, so I didn't worry about it anymore. At the same time I got the call my Dad was rushed to the hospital I didn't know if he had another stroke or a heart attack. Turned out he had bleeding ulcers due to his medication. My Dad had been saying for a few years he wasn't going to live much longer. I kept telling him to watch what you say about yourself, you keep declaring it, it probably will happen. When I saw him in ICU he told me straight up he wasn't going to make it out of there. I told him he could make it, but when your 75 years old and you've had four or five strokes and you can't drive anymore and you can't go fishing or work in the wood shop it made it hard for him to not want to get better. He pretty much had a death wish, he quit eating and starved his self to death and went into a coma and me and my mother just watched him decline rather rapidly. He passed away May 7th a week before my birthday on the 14th. During this time no one knew I slept like three days in my vehicle; again my ole friend Sallie called me and as we were talking she pulled out of me where I had been living, she couldn't believe it and just told me to come and stay with her and her husband for as long as I needed to save money. They allowed me to stay with them for six months. It was a huge blessing for the both of us. Sallie had just went through major surgery to remove cancer and found out at the same time she had 4 stage Cirrhosis of the liver as well. I was able to help with cooking and lite cleaning helping with the laundry that kind of stuff and they helped me by letting me be there and save up money to get a head and in looking for a townhouse to purchase. The Lord reminded me that He told me He had many dwelling places and I was believing it too! The Lord was opening up doors for me for His provision and I was coming into the real knowledge that He was my Father, even more now since my Dad had passed away. My Dad wasn't perfect but my Heavenly Father was. He was just about to bless me more that I could ever imagined.

It wasn't too long after all this that a friend text me to come to a healing service and to invite my friend Sallie maybe she could get prayed for and possibly get healed. Well I had just started working night shift at work so I texted her back and let know I could not make it. The next couple of days went by and she called me again to say I had to meet her for dinner, she wanted to tell me about the church meeting she had invited me to. Well, we met and she told me about this church in Dalton, Georgia that was seeing a true sign and wonder. How a man's Bible was dripping with oil, she told me to look it up on Youtube and see what I thought. Then she told me she had some of that oil and wanted to share it with me and to use it to anoint Sallie and myself and see if anything changed, for many people were getting healed from rare disease and people who were unemployed were getting jobs. I looked it up on Youtube listen to the testimonies and I took the oil my friend had given me and put it on myself and Sallie and we both prayed for each other.

The next week Sallie went and got her blood checked and saw the nurse about her liver. The doctor told her it looked like her liver was trying to heal itself…we don't see this ever. So she was so excited and her energy level had increased tremendously to where she hadn't been out of the house for over a year and now she was able to stay on the go for days at a time, even more she was starting to do some of the cooking and laundry too. We were all amazed. I even started to feel better, the nerve pain I was experiencing had gone away from my feet. Then not only that a window in Heaven had opened above me and great great provisions started to pour out for me to receive. My Mom called me and told me she wanted to pay off my SUV for me which was about four thousand dollars, she said I think that will help you in the long run don't you think? I said, Mom it will help in the short run too! Wasn't too long and I found a Townhouse I would like to buy, found out it was a foreclosure, the bank owned it and had done all the updates to it, new painting and flooring with a new stove and dish washer too. Mom saw it and liked it as well, she had told me months ago she would help me by getting a bedroom suit for me.

Since I moved back from Oklahoma I didn't have any furniture. Then she let me know she was going to buy me a refridgerator and washer and dryer also.

Then unexpectantly two weeks before closing my SUV brokedown on me. I remember jumping out of it and declaring out loud to the enemy, he could not sucker punch me and shouting you did it now, you just set me up for a blessing and you don't evern know it, because this vehicle belongs to The Lord, so I got my car over to the mechanic's shop and they told me it was bad news, I told them I was closing on a house in three weeks this is not perfect timing. I didn't want payments again either. My mom came to rescue me and she let me use her car for a day to go and find me something I could buy. So I beat the hedges down looking all over the place and I found a certified Honda car. When I called Mom from the dealership, she told me she wanted to buy it for me so I wouldn't have to worry about a car payment or insurance. That was a huge blessing I was so shocked at her for wanting to do this for me. My mom was so gracious to me when I told my friends they too were shocked. I told them, "I think my mom must of gotten saved"! She has never done anything like this for me in my entire life. I am so grateful that I know the Lord had a hand in this by softening my mom's heart and wanting to help me get established in a home of my own. I think she was truly worried about me and wanted me to get settled. I think she thought I might go back to Oklahoma too. But I know I can't move that far away and leave her by herself, her health is not the best at this time, so I felt I need to stay close to home.

So, as it is now, I have experience the Love of the Father like I have never known. He has protected me, provided for me and He has affirmed me, that I am a child, very loved and known by Him, His ridiculous grace has set me free in many many areas of my life and I feel like I live out of a place that I now belong to, I have been called to a seat at the table and I sit right by the Savior, Jesus and it's a very safe and comfortable place in His presence where I belong.

If you want go to Youtube and listen to the song "come to the table", its perfect to this chapter of my life. Hopefully if you feel like you'er suffering from the mindset of an Orphan you too can come in out of those lies and hear the truth that you are loved and you as well have a seat saved by the Savior right by Him!

THE END

This is Tom with Garth, one of his favorite pets

This is the picture we used for Tom's memorial

2005 when I was a Service Writer for a Buick GMC Pontiac dealer

This is Casper Tom, my Schnauzer who I often dressed up and photographed.

this is Me in 2013 doing my favorite thing: photography

Easter Sunday April 5, 2015 at Church of the Highlands, Woodlawn Campus.

Pastor Aldger Armstead baptizing me, I HAVE DECIDED TO FOLLOW JESUS!

Taking a "Selfie" of me from the 60th floor of the Towers. 2016

This is my New Identity in Christ, God my Father has changed me from the Inside out, and given me beauty for ashes. (2017)

www.ingramcontent.com/pod-product-compliance
Lightning Source LLC
Chambersburg PA
CBHW051315120626
46547CB00015B/2246